THE BEST OF
LIVERPOOL

THE BEST OF
LIVERPOOL

First published in the UK in 2007

Updated and reprinted in 2019

© G2 Entertainment Ltd 2019

www.G2ent.co.uk

Printed and bound printed in Europe

ISBN 978-1-782816-51-5

The views in this book are those of the author but they are general views only and readers are urged to consult the relevant and qualified specialist for individual advice in particular situations. G2 Entertainment Limited hereby exclude all liability to the extent permitted by law of any errors or omissions in this book and for any loss, damage or expense (whether direct or indirect) suffered by a third party relying on any information contained in this book.

All our best endeavours have been made to secure copyright clearance for every photograph used but in the event of any copyright owner being overlooked please address correspondence to G2 Entertainment, Unit 16, Beaufort Road, Reigate, Surrey, RH2 9DJ

Contents

Alexander-Arnold

Liverpool born lad who won the Champions League when he was only 20. A superb attacking right back whose ability to fizz in crosses with perfect pace and trajectory makes him an essential part of the Reds attacking machine, as illustrated when providing a hat-trick of assists in a February 2019 win over Watford. This was during a season in which his 12 assists were a record for a defender.

That ability on the ball is also shown with his prowess at free kicks, his first goal coming from a dead ball on his European debut in a Champions League fixture with Hoffenheim.

Having been part of Liverpool's Academy since 2004 Trent had been well tutored so that by the time he achieved his first team debut as an 18-year old there had been 12 years of investment in his future by Liverpool's staff.

Young Player of the Year two years running from 2017, in 2018 he became Liverpool's youngest Champions League finalist. While that occasion ended in disappointment there was to be delight 12 months later when triumph in Madrid came as Trent became the youngest man to start consecutive Champions League finals.

Attacking full backs need to be part of a system that protects them when they can get caught up-field but Alexander-Arnold's defensive calibre was amply illustrated when awarded the Man of the Match award in an April 2018 Champions League victory over Manchester City where Liverpool's clean sheet was in no small part due to Trent's taming of City winger Leroy Sane.

Capped by England when still a teenager, he played at the 2018 World Cup and seems set to have a long career for club and country.

Aldridge

John Aldridge may only have been at Anfield for a short time, but after scoring 63 goals in just 104 games, he is considered one of the best goal-scorers to wear the red jersey.

Aldridge, or 'Aldo' as he is affectionately known, was signed by Liverpool in January 1987 for £750 000 in order to fill the boots of the soon to be departed Ian Rush.

He grew up supporting the Reds and certainly became a crowd favourite during the two and a half years he spent at the club. The born and bred Scouser began his career at amateur side South Liverpool before signing for Newport County, where his impressive goal scoring record attracted the attention of Oxford United, for whom he signed in March 1984.

The arrival of Aldridge coincided with a period of success for United as

they enjoyed promotion from the Third Division to the First in the space of three years - and their top scorer certainly caught the eye of Kenny Dalglish. The new boy got his Liverpool career off to a dream start by scoring the only goal of the game on his full debut against Southampton in February 1987.

It was the following season that the Republic of Ireland international truly left his mark as he scored nine goals in the first nine games of the season. He was an integral part of Liverpool's 1987-88 Championship winning side - scoring 26 league goals as the team went 29 games without defeat.

final the following season and extinguished any bad memories by opening the scoring in a 3-2 win.

At the beginning of the 1989-90 season Real Sociedad made a £1.1 million offer for Liverpool's No.8 and he departed for Spain in September 1989 - but not before scoring a penalty in a 9-0 win against Crystal Palace in his last game for the club.

His goal-scoring exploits continued in Spain and he became a fans' favourite at the Basque side. After two years Aldridge returned to Merseyside when he signed for Tranmere Rovers and equalled the club's goal scoring record in his first season - netting 40 goals in total.

He became player-manager at Prenton Park and hung up his boots in 1998 with 474 goals in 882 games, overtaking Jimmy Greaves as British football's record goal scorer. He was honoured with a benefit match against the Liverpool side of 1987-88.

His Tranmere side got to the Worthington Cup final in 2000 but lost out narrowly to Leicester City. The following season, with Tranmere struggling in the bottom half of Division One, Aldridge resigned as manager. He now works in the media and is a regular pundit on LFC TV.

The season ended on a sour note for the striker, though, as Liverpool lost out on claiming a league and cup double. Aldo became the first player to miss a penalty in a FA Cup final at Wembley as the Reds were beaten by giant-killing Wimbledon.

Thankfully, Aldridge returned to Wembley for the Merseyside FA Cup

Alisson

Needing a new goalkeeper after Loris Karius' performance in the 2018 Champions League final, Jurgen Klopp took characteristically decisive action. A world record fee for a keeper of a reported £66.8m was spent on acquiring Brazilian international Alisson Becker from Roma. The signing quickly proved astute as he won the Premier League's Golden Gloves award with 21 clean sheets, having played every minute of the 38 game domestic league season.

Playing for Liverpool you have to be an attacking threat no matter your position and in Alisson the Reds acquired a player who is so often the base of the attack, his positive and penetrating distribution starting many a move.

Born in Novo, Hamburgo, in Brazil on 2 October 1992 Alisson began in his home country with Internacional before joining Roma in the summer of 2016. Initially back up to ex-Arsenal keeper Wojciech Szczesny he debuted in the Champions League against Porto and went on to help the Giallorossi to the semi-finals in his second season when he impressed against Liverpool.

All-time Attendance Records

For comparison's sake, the capacity of today's all-seater Anfield is 54,074; figures in excess of this were of course established when both ends of the ground were standing terraces.

HIGHEST LEAGUE ATTENDANCE: 58,757 v Chelsea (1949)

HIGHEST FA CUP ATTENDANCE: 61,905 v Wolves (1952) fifth round

HIGHEST LEAGUE CUP ATTENDANCE: 53,051 v Tottenham Hotspur (2016) Fourth Round

HIGHEST EUROPEAN ATTENDANCE: 55,104 v Barcelona (1976) semi-final second leg

LOWEST FA CUP ATTENDANCE (POST-WAR): 11,207 v Chester City, 1945-46 third round second leg

LOWEST LEAGUE ATTENDANCE: 1,000 v Loughborough Town (1895)

LOWEST LEAGUE ATTENDANCE: (POST-WAR) 11,976 v Scunthorpe United (1959) Division 2

LOWEST FA CUP ATTENDANCE: 4,000 v Newton (1892) second qualifying round

LOWEST LEAGUE CUP ATTENDANCE: 9,902 v Brentford (1983) second round second leg

LOWEST EUROPEAN ATTENDANCE: 12,021 Dundalk (1982) European Cup first round first leg

All-time Team

1   Ray Clemence
2   Chris Lawler
3   Emlyn Hughes
4   Virgil Van Dijk
5   Ron Yeats
6   Graeme Souness
7   Kevin Keegan
8   Ian Rush
9   Kenny Dalglish
10   Steven Gerrard
11   Billy Liddell

Subs

12   Alisson
13   Alan Hansen
14   Michael Owen
15   Ian St. John
16   Roger Hunt
17   Ian Callaghan
18   Mo Salah

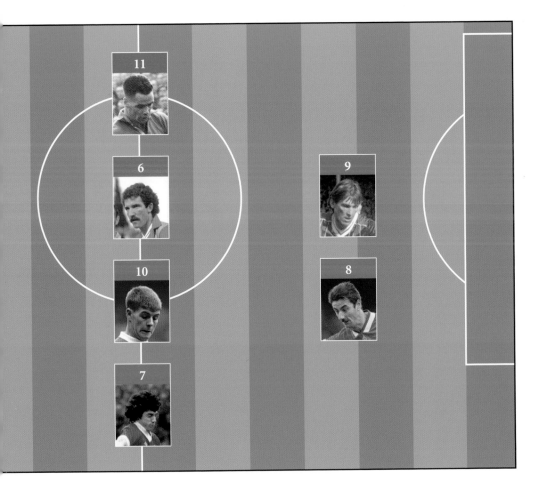

RIGHT Liverpool play to a capacity crowd at Anfield

BELOW The famous players tunnel at Anfield

Anfield

Anfield is, in many ways, the key to the continued success of the team that plays there. A sign over the tunnel leading from the dressing rooms to the pitch reminds visitors that 'This Is Anfield' – a warning that's superfluous the moment opposing players feel the grass beneath their boots. Because the vocal support Liverpool's fans have given their team over the years is second to none.

Go back to 1884, of course, and it was Everton that originally inhabited the embryonic stadium, moving across to Stanley Park in 1892 - since which time it's been red through and through!

The whole tradition of community singing and terrace chanting developed on the Kop which became all-seater in 1994, eleven years after the Anfield Road terrace had become seated.

Two years before that, an upper tier had been added to the Kemlyn Road stand, which thereby became the Centenary Stand. A similar second tier was added to the Anfield Road stand in 1998, bringing the capacity up to an impressive 45,362.

Even that wasn't sufficient for the demand to see the Reds and in 2016 the opening of the newly extended main stand lifted Anfield's capacity to over 54,000 with the club ambitious to continue extending even further.

Other additions to the ground to highlight significant people and events have included the Shankly Gates, erected in 1982 in memory of the legendary manager Bill Shankly, who had passed away the previous year; the Paisley Gateway, erected outside the Kop in 1999 in honour of the club's most successful manager ever; and the eternal flame of the Hillsborough Memorial, dedicated to the 96 fans who so tragically lost their lives in 1989.

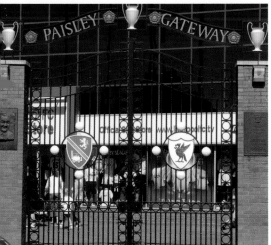

Anfield has been used to host international games, most notably the Scotland versus Wales World Cup qualifier in 1977, and, while Goodison Park was Merseyside's World Cup venue in 1966 when England hosted the final stages, it was Anfield that, 30 years later, hosted four games in Euro '96 (Eire and Holland having already met in a qualifying play-off). But then Anfield had staged its first international, between England and Ireland, as far back as 1889!

ABOVE Anfield viewed from the outside

LEFT Paisley Gateway entrance at Anfield

Barnes

Jamaican-born John Barnes, the son of a diplomat, came into this world on 7 November 1963. He was a sensational goalscorer with Watford, helping them climb to the top division, before he moved to Anfield for a then-record £900,000 fee in 1987.

Already capped by England, his international performances had not gone uncriticised, although he had scored one magnificent goal in Brazil's Maracana Stadium. Altogether, he was to play 79 times in an England shirt, a total that speaks for itself.

Manager Kenny Dalglish was convinced that Barnes would be a considerable asset to his side, and to begin with he certainly was: he scored 61 goals in his first four seasons, mainly from midfield, and he helped Liverpool to two League championships, the FA Cup and the League Cup. He slowed up a bit as

time went on but he could still be effective as a midfield anchor.

Barnes left for Newcastle United in August 1997, but by then his playing career was drawing to its close. Following limited and unsuccessful club managerial experience at Celtic and Tranmere Rovers, as well as time in charge of the Jamaican national side, he has established himself as a competent and likeable television presenter.

LEFT Barnes in action for Liverpool against Sheffield Wednesday, 1995

BELOW Barnes takes on Robert Lee of Newcastle, 1994

BELOW RIGHT
Beardsley goes past
Gary Pallister of
Manchester United
during the FA Charity
Shield of 1990

BELOW Beardsley in
action for Liverpool

Beardsley

In terms of star quality, Peter Beardsley was a late developer.

Born in Newcastle in 1961, he began his professional career with Carlisle United in 1979, but he then wandered between Vancouver Whitecaps and Manchester United (for whom he made no League appearances) until he signed for his hometown club in 1983. There, along with Kevin Keegan and Chris Waddle, his predatory striking skills helped Newcastle gain promotion to the top flight.

The diminutive striker had arrived, and in time he was to play for his country on 59 occasions. Following some exuberant appearances in the 1986 World Cup, Beardsley was signed by Kenny Dalglish in July 1987 for £1.9 million.

He soon began knocking in the goals for his new club. Although he scored 46 times in 131 league games, Dalglish often left him out of the side after his first season, and when Graeme Souness took over as manager he sold Beardsley to Everton for £1 million.

Peter Beardsley was wandering once more. After two years at Everton, he went back to Newcastle, where he was welcomed as a returning hero – and scored another 47 League goals. Before hanging up his boots, he played for Bolton Wanderers, Manchester City, Fulham, Hartlepool United, Doncaster Rovers and Melbourne Knights, and has subsequently pursued a career in coaching.

Benitez

He was hailed as a Spanish messiah, a genial tactician who restored Liverpool's reputation as one of Europe's biggest clubs and led the team to one of the greatest triumphs in its history.

But after a six-year reign of cup glory and league frustration Rafael Benitez's hopes of leading Liverpool to a record-breaking 19th League Championship were brought to an end following a disappointing 2009-10 campaign.

The Spaniard's first year in England ended like a fairytale, capped by a European achievement that will ensure his tenure will be immortalised and cherished in the annals of Anfield history.

Following his departure from the club Rafa made a donation of £96,000 to the Hillsborough Family Support Group, a mark of the man's class. Having managed Valencia amongst a host of Spanish clubs before becoming the first Spanish manager to manage in the Premier League when he came to Liverpool, after departing the club Benitez CV took in Inter, Chelsea, Real Madrid, and Newcastle before he moved to China with Dalian Yifang in 2019.

ABOVE Rafael Benitez gestures as Chelsea's caretaker manager Guus Hiddink looks on

ABOVE Ronnie Moran, caretaker-manager for Liverpool in 1991

RIGHT An emotional Roy Evans shakes hands with Liverpool chairman David Moores as he leaves the club after 33 years' service, signalling the end of the boot room tradition in 1998

Boot Room

The Anfield 'boot room', where the coaching staff met to plot future games over a cup of tea or, occasionally, something stronger, would become a notable breeding ground for future Liverpool bosses.

Bob Paisley, though almost unknown outside Liverpool when he took the management job on in 1974 (some claim against his better judgement), had been a valued member of Bill Shankly's boot room team, and would go on to eclipse even 'Shanks' in terms of trophies won.

Boot room regular Joe Fagan would hold the reins briefly from 1983 to 1985, his successful spell soured by the tragic events of Heysel.

When Kenny Dalglish, elevated from player to manager, quit in 1989 after Hillsborough, caretaker manager Ronnie Moran emerged from the boot room to lead the team to a morale-boosting 7-1 win at Derby.

BOOT ROOM

Another former player and boot room regular, Phil Thompson, became Houllier's assistant, taking over during his heart scare, but the Frenchman effectively closed the boot room, although many of its traditions live on at the club.

Roy Evans became assistant to incoming manager Graeme Souness, and when things fell apart in early 1994, he was on hand to pick up the pieces. Unfortunately, little was achieved during his reign and the arrival of Gérard Houllier, initially in a joint managerial capacity, was the beginning of the end. Nevertheless, the unassuming ex-full back had contributed greatly to Liverpool's success over the years.

Callaghan

'Cally', just turned 18, was applauded off the field by his teammates after his first-team debut for Liverpool – against Bristol Rovers in April 1960 – and went on to rack up applause, awards and medals galore in a marathon career at Anfield. Born on 10 April 1942, Ian Callaghan was the only Liverpool player to appear for them during their Second Division days and still be there as the European Cup was hoisted in 1977. A direct right-winger in his early days but later used in midfield, Cally comfortably became the

holder of the club's appearance record, playing 857 times – almost 200 clear of Emlyn Hughes and Ray Clemence – before moving to Swansea in 1978. He ended his career at Crewe Alexandra in 1982.

He scored 69 goals for the Reds, 49 of them in the league. Once Liverpool, and Ian Callaghan, had won the Second Division championship in 1961-62, they went from strength to strength, winning five First Division titles, the FA Cup twice, the UEFA Cup twice plus the European Cup and European Super Cup. And on a personal level, Callaghan was the football writers' Player of the Year in 1974 and was awarded the MBE.

He played four times for England, twice in the early stages of the 1966 World Cup competition, but curiously had to wait another eleven years before gaining his third cap.

Carragher

Jamie Carragher is quite simply a living legend at the club after 17 years of outstanding service.

A one-club man, he was Liverpool's vice-captain for 10 years, and is the club's second-longest ever serving player, making his 737th appearance for Liverpool in all competitions on 19 May 2013.

Carragher – or 'Carra' as he was affectionately known - also holds the record for the most appearances in European competition for Liverpool with 150 games.

Carragher started his footballing career at the Liverpool Academy, making his professional debut in the 1996-97 season when he scored a rare goal against Aston Villa at Anfield.

He became a first team regular at full-back the following season but with the arrival of manager Rafael Benitez in 2004, he moved to centre-back, where he remained for the rest of his career.

His honours with Liverpool include two FA Cups, three League Cups, one UEFA Cup and one Champions League when the club came back from 3-0 down at half-time to win against AC Milan.

Internationally, Carragher held the national record for most caps at under-21 level and earned his senior debut in 1999. He represented England at the 2004 European Championship and the

BELOW Carragher vies with Robbie Keane of Spurs

CARRAGHER

BELOW Carragher scores in the penalty shoot-out during the Worthington Cup Final match against Birmingham City, 2001

2006 World Cup before announcing his retirement from international football in 2007.

He did, however, temporarily come out of retirement in order to represent England at the 2010 World Cup before retiring again with 38 senior England caps.

Since finishing his playing days Jamie has become a high profile pundit on Sky Sports.

Case

Tough-tackling, hard-working midfielder Jimmy Case (born on 18 May 1954) arrived at Anfield in May 1973 for a bargain £500 from non-league South Liverpool. Over the following eight seasons he topped 250 appearances and scored 46 goals, many of them thunderous efforts from outside the penalty area.

After making his debut on the final day of the 1974-75 season, Case made 39 first team appearances in all in 1975-76. He helped Liverpool to the UEFA Cup that season, weighing in with all three home goals as Slask Wroclaw of Poland were beaten 5-1. His intervention proved crucial in the final against Club Brugge, too. Liverpool, two down inside 12 minutes of the home leg, sent on Case for John Toshack and he inspired a magnificent comeback, scoring the Reds' second goal in a 3-2 success. A 1-1 draw in the second leg meant a second UEFA Cup success for Liverpool.

At Wembley in 1977 he scored with a wonderful shot on the turn to equalise against Manchester United in the FA Cup Final.

LEFT Case playing for Liverpool in the Charity Shield, 1979

BELOW Jimmy Case in action during a match against Everton at Anfield in 1977

Over the next few seasons, Case linked well with Graeme Souness, Terry McDermott and Ray Kennedy in the Reds' engine room before being ousted in 1980-81 by Sammy Lee. By this time he had, among others, three European Cup medals and four league championship medals to show for his efforts.

Case moved to Brighton, a club he later managed, in the summer of 1981. His final retirement came at the grand old age of 41.

Champions League / European Cup

BELOW RIGHT Liverpool celebrate victory over Bruges in 1978

BELOW A European lap of honour after beating Borussia Moenchengladbach, 1977

Since 1977 when Kevin Keegan and co first brought the European Cup to Merseyside no club have been champions of Europe more times than the Reds. When Jordan Henderson lifted the Champions League trophy in 2019 it was the sixth time Liverpool had been the top team on the continent. The only club that can match Liverpool are Real Madrid who have also been European Cup / Champions League winners six times between Liverpool's first and sixth titles. However, in that time Real have been in fewer finals than Liverpool, the men from Anfield also having been runners' up three times in that time compared to Real's once – in their case losing to Liverpool in their own city in 1981.

During this fabulous period from 1977 to 2019 when Liverpool won the European Cup / Champions League in 1977, 1978, 1981, 1984, 2005 and 2019 AC Milan and Barcelona each won the

trophy four times while Bayern Munich; whose golden period was immediately before Liverpool's first triumph, reached seven finals in the 1977-2019 period but won only two of them.

Since the European Cup began in 1955-56 (It changed to the Champions League in 1992-93) only Real Madrid and AC Milan have been continental champions more times than Liverpool (To 2019), while the next most successful English club have won only half as many titles as Liverpool.

Winning the Champions League in 2019 was a glorious triumph and one that contained many more stories than simply winning the final. Indeed, the final was one of the more comfortable games of the campaign. Ahead in only the second minute thanks to a penalty tucked away by Mo Salah, Liverpool were always in control against a Tottenham team in their first final, with Divock Origi putting the seal on the win with a clinical late finish.

The semi-final was incredible. Beaten 3-0 in the first leg in Barcelona the second leg looked like a formality for the Catalan side with Reds fans hoping for the miracle of miracles and a European night to match the greatest in the tra-

dition of supreme European nights at Anfield. They couldn't could they? They could! Somehow, spectacularly, wonderfully Liverpool defeated the much admired Barcelona – Lionel Messi and all – 4-0 and therefore 4-3 on aggregate.

Origi made an early breakthrough after just seven minutes but Barca looked comfortable eight minutes into the second half when there had been no further reduction in their advantage. Step forward Gini Wijnaldum. His two goals in three minutes transformed the tie and meant that hoped for miracle had arrived. Suddenly Barcelona, a team who must have thought they had seen and done everything found themselves walking through a storm as their dreams were tossed and blown. A Liverpool winner seemed inevitable and with 11 minutes to go Origi joined Wijnaldum in netting his second goal of the

ABOVE Steven Gerrard proudly lifts the Champions League trophy in 2005

game. Incredibly Liverpool were in the final. It was the performance of true champions but not the first of the campaign.

While the quarter-final had brought handsome home and away victories over Porto the round of 16 had needed a superb display in Germany where a brace from Sadio Mane combined with a goal from Virgil Van Dijk had produced a 3-1 win at Bayern Munich following Liverpool being held to a goalless draw at Anfield.

It was a much needed away performance following three defeats out of three away from home in the group stage. Only a narrow home win over Napoli at Anfield in the final group game had edged the Reds through ahead of Napoli who had the same number of points and the same goal difference.

Liverpool's first venture into Europe came in the European Cup of 1964-65 after winning their first League title under Bill Shankly. In this competition they were defeated by Inter Milan in the San Siro by 3-0, having won the first leg 3-1. So near yet so far!

Liverpool's record was a model of consistency, qualifying for Europe for 21 consecutive seasons (1964-65 to 1984-85) until the post-Heysel ban. It was a Liverpool trademark that the first team was backed up by an able squad of reserves ready to step in at a moment's notice, and it was this strength in depth that helped them obtain such consistent success.

Liverpool's victory in 2005 was their fifth European Cup (Champions League) success. The first came in 1977, when Bob Paisley's team beat Borussia Moenchengladbach in Rome. Paisley's team talk consisted of the story of him rolling into Rome on the back of a tank as part of the liberating forces – and thanks to goals from Terry McDermott, Tommy Smith (a rare strike from the veteran defender) and a Phil Neal penalty they liberated the silverware from, er, German hands!

The following season saw them retain their trophy, a single-goal win against Bruges at Wembley that was functional rather than entertaining. With Kevin Keegan now out of the picture at Hamburg, the Kopites found a new hero in Celtic's Kenny Dalglish. He chipped an unforgettable winner from a Souness through ball to take the title.

Three years then passed until Liverpool travelled to Paris to face the mighty Real Madrid, the team with the best European Cup pedigree of them all. Stalemate ruled until, with six minutes left on the clock, the Kennedys, Ray and Alan, combined. Surprisingly it was striker turned midfielder Ray whose quick throw-in sent Alan away to net, but who cared when the result was a Cup hat-trick?

The last European Cup win Liverpool were to register for 21 years came in 1984, against Roma on penalties. Since then there's been the unforgettable comeback from 3-0 down to secure another penalty win in 2005 against AC Milan in Istanbul, and the 2007 final against the same opposition.

Liverpool were beaten 3-1 by Real Madrid in Moscow in the 2018 final in Kiev when Sadio Mane's goal wasn't enough on a night when Mo Salah limped out of the action after only a third of it. A goal from Karim Benzema combined with a brace from Gareth Bale ended Liverpool's hopes on an awful night for 'keeper Loris Karius but 12 months later Liverpool were back in style as once again they were crowned the Kings of Europe as befits European Royalty.

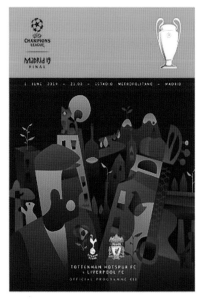

LEFT Official match programme for the 2019 UEFA Champions League Final

Charity / Community Shield

The FA Charity Shield (now called the Community Shield) is the traditional curtain-raiser to the English domestic football campaign, played between the winners of the league's top division and the FA Cup. The first Charity Shield match, played in 1908 between Manchester United and Queens Park Rangers, was a professionals-versus-amateurs affair.

The match was moved to coincide with the start of the new season in 1959, and has kept its place in the football calendar ever since.

In 1974, FA secretary Ted Croker proposed the annual match should be played at Wembley as the official foretaste of the season. It was Liverpool who celebrated this upgrade with a 6-5 penalty shoot-out win against Leeds United after the 90 minutes had finished in a 1-1 draw. The match was memorable for the uncharitable behaviour of Billy Bremner and Kevin Keegan, who both made history by being sent off for indulging in fisticuffs. (After that, teams finishing level shared the Shield for six months apiece before the penalty shoot-out was reintroduced in 1993.)

Liverpool have won the Charity Shield 15 times, in 1964 (shared), 1965 (shared), 1966, 1974, 1976, 1977 (shared), 1979, 1980, 1982, 1986 (shared), 1988, 1989 1990 (shared), 2001 and 2006.

Clemence

Given that Ray Clemence was in time to become one of England's greatest goal-keepers, it is perhaps surprising that he was initially press-ganged into putting on the jersey by his school sports master.

Born in Skegness on 5 August 1948, he preferred playing in the outfield, but he took to goalkeeping well enough to be offered trials by Notts County and Scunthorpe United – where he was paid £11 a week, and later attracted the attention of Bill Shankly. He made his League debut for Liverpool in 1970, when Tommy Lawrence was injured.

In terms of honours earned, his Liverpool debut marked the start of one of the most successful careers in modern football. Playing behind one of the best-organised defences in the country, between 1971 and 1981 Clemence helped his side to the League Championship five times, the FA Cup, the League Cup, the European

BELOW Clemence catches the ball in mid-air, 1975

Cup (three times) and the UEFA Cup (twice). He also earned a runners-up medal in two FA Cup Finals and in the League Cup. He was to play a total of 666 games for Liverpool in all competitions, and in 1978-79 he set a First Division record when he conceded just 16 goals in 42 games.

Clemence was lithe and supple, and able to reach the most difficult of shots. He was one of the first goalkeepers to act as an additional sweeper, by moving outside the penalty area before the opposing forward could get to the ball.

Had it not been for the presence of Peter Shilton, he would have played in far more than the 61 internationals he

graced over an 11-year period. As it was, he kept 27 clean sheets in those 61 matches, during a period when the England side was not at its best. In all, he played in 12 World Cup qualifying matches but never got near to playing in a World Cup Final. It was a similar story when it came to European Championship matches, although Clemence did feature in two games played in the 1980 finals in Italy.

Before his international career drew to a close, Clemence moved to Tottenham Hotspur. He was 33 years old and the move surprised many. He was far from finished, however. He played more than 300 games for Spurs, helping them lift the FA Cup in 1982.

Raymond Neal Clemence OBE retired due to injury during the 1987-88 season, having played in a remarkable total of 1,119 matches.

Dalglish

Nobody who has heard him speak will be surprised to learn that Kenny Dalglish comes from Glasgow. Having been born there in 1951, he joined Celtic and made more than 200 appearances for the Bhoys before moving to Anfield in August 1977 as a replacement for Kevin Keegan. Bob Paisley knew he had a bargain. "His genius is not only in his own ability but in making others play," he said.

Dour and uncommunicative off the field, Dalglish seemed to have an entirely different personality when he was playing. Though he failed to score on his debut, the goalless Charity Shield clash with Manchester United, he would notch 118 league goals in red, 172 first team goals in total, as well as making countless more for others. His 1978 European Cup-winning strike against Bruges at Wembley capped a sensational first season, and he was not to disappoint thereafter. International honours continued, too. In all, he was capped 102 times by Scotland, 54 of these coming while at Anfield.

During June 1985, before the end of an outstanding career as a Liverpool player (during which time he featured in 355 league games and picked up enough medals to fill a couple of bedside cabinets), Dalglish took over as player-manager.

If anyone was worried about his mastery of the transfer market, the acquisition of the likes of John Barnes, Peter Beardsley and Jamie Redknapp proved those concerns misplaced. And John Aldridge was bought to replace Ian Rush, just as Dalglish had replaced Keegan.

Liverpool won the Double the following season, and went on to win two

more League titles while Dalglish was at the helm, fellow Scot Alan Hansen his captain and voice on the pitch. It was therefore to the dismay of many Reds fans that 'King Kenny' quit the manager's job in 1991, claiming the stress factor was too great.

His sudden departure mirrored that

of fellow Scot and legend Bill Shankly, but the strain of Hillsborough and its aftermath (in which he played an unsung part consoling the bereaved) was clearly a contributory factor.

An enigmatic character, Dalglish was soon managing again, this time at Blackburn Rovers, where he successfully teamed up with the late Ray Harford, and later at Newcastle United and Celtic. He returned to Liverpool in 2009 with a role within Rafa Benitez's backroom set-up and was warmly welcomed back into the Anfield family. Before the appointment of Roy Hodgson as manager in July 2010, there was even talk of King Kenny returning to the Liverpool hot seat.

But in January 2011, at the age of 59, new owners Fenway Sports Group brought him back to the Anfield helm almost two decades after his resignation, assuming an interim position as Red's boss following the departure of Roy Hodgson by mutual consent.

His impact was an instant one as the team quickly ascended from the lower reaches of the table in to the top half. And in the following season he steered his side to a Carling Cup success over Cardiff City at Wembley, ending the club's six-year wait for silverware and securing a return to European football for 2012-13.

Liverpool also reached the FA Cup final, where they narrowly lost out to Chelsea, however it was the league form which ultimately led to the announcement he would cease to manage his beloved team on May 16, 2012.

What 'King Kenny' accomplished as both a player and manager for Liverpool Football Club may never be matched again; and he is still a welcome guest at home matches for the rest of his life. In 2017 the Centenary Stand at Anfield was renamed in his honour. He was knighted in 2018.

Derby Matches

ABOVE Steven Gerrard is shown the red card after his foul on Everton's Kevin Campbell (on the ground) in 1999

Local derbies are, by definition, hard-fought affairs. Whether you're in Manchester, Glasgow, London or Liverpool, no quarter will be given and no prisoners taken. Yet few derby matches are played in the same uniquely humorous spirit as the Merseyside clash between Liverpool and Everton.

The city's penchant for ready wit is well chronicled, having turned out a wealth of professional funnymen from Jimmy Tarbuck to Alexei Sayle. But on derby day, every one of the supporters packed into Goodison Park or Anfield is ready and willing to add their own page to the history of the fixture.

The first League derby between the teams took place at Goodison Park on 13 October 1894, and it was the Blues who drew first blood in a 3-0 win. The return saw honours even at 2-2, but Liverpool found the First Division some-what inhospitable and subsided into the

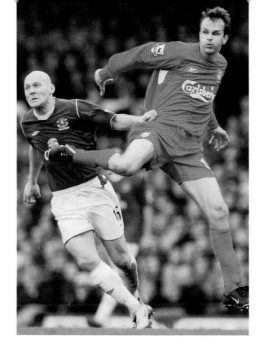

relegation zone, and a single-goal reverse against Bury saw them relegated.

A 106-goal record haul took the Reds back up with some ease in 1896, putting the Merseyside derby back on the agenda. And that, give or take the odd season, is exactly where it's been for Liverpool and Everton supporters for the century and more that's followed.

The 1980s onwards have seen many different nationalities. It should be remembered, though, that the very first team Liverpool fielded in 1892 contained not one Merseysider … in fact, all eleven members of the 'team of the macs' were Scots! So Liverpool v Everton derbies have always had their cosmopolitan side.

The 1980s also brought two FA Cup Final meetings, both of which are profiled in detail elsewhere.

In the long history of Merseyside derbies, which game has been the greatest of all time? Many people's money will be on the FA Cup Fifth Round replay of 1991. The 4-4 draw had a sensational sting in the tail when Anfield legend Kenny Dalglish revealed it was his last match in charge. Ironically, it would be the man who succeeded him, Graeme Souness, who ran into heart problems, because this pulsating 120 minutes had absolutely everything. Suffice to say that four Liverpool goals found four Everton ripostes, confirming, if confirmation were needed, that the Merseyside derby remained one of football's most passionately contested fixtures.

LEFT Thomas Gravesen of Everton battles for the ball with Dietmar Hamann, 2004

BELOW Adrian Heath of Everton jumps to head the ball as Alan Hansen looks on, 1984

ABOVE Jerzy Dudek
faces Pirlo of AC Milan
in the penalty shoot-
out, Champions League
Final 2005

BELOW Dudek then
saves the decisive
penalty from AC Milan
forward Shevchenko

Dudek

Signed from Dutch club Feyenoord in the summer of 2001 for £5.5 million to replace the error-prone Sander Westerveld, Polish international Jerzy Dudek (born on 23 March 1973) had played 136 games for the Dutch side after joining from Sokol Tychy and established himself as first choice for his country. He had the misfortune, however, to join Liverpool in a relatively fallow period, and also to make a few televised howlers.

Despite figuring for Poland in the 2002 World Cup, the League Cup in 2003 was his only honour in the red (or should that be green) of Liverpool until the 2005 Champions League Final gave him the platform to put on a match-winning performance in what was billed as his final game for the Reds.

He lost his starting position to Pepe Reina following an arm injury before departing to Real Madrid at the end of the 2006-07 season but is still warmly regarded by Liverpool fans, who voted him number 36 in the list of 100 Players Who Shook The Kop.

FA Cup

Liverpool had to wait until 1914 to contest their first Cup Final, and were unfortunate to lose by a single goal to fellow Lancashire outfit Burnley. The FA Cup would prove an unlucky competition for the Reds, and it wasn't until 1950 that they'd reach the Final again. By now it was at Wembley, and they journeyed

ABOVE Liverpool win the FA Cup in 2006, with Steve Gerrard very much hero of the day!

LEFT Liverpool in the FA Cup Final of 1914 against Burnley played at Crystal Palace

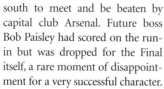

RIGHT Led by Alan
Hansen, Liverpool
celebrate FA Cup
victory in 1986

BELOW Captain of
Liverpool, Ron Yeats
holds the Cup as he
is chaired by fellow
members of the
victorious team, 1965

south to meet and be beaten by capital club Arsenal. Future boss Bob Paisley had scored on the run-in but was dropped for the Final itself, a rare moment of disappointment for a very successful character.

But defeat at Wembley in 1950 preceded relegation four years later, and the first win would not occur until well into the Shankly reign. But the victory in 1965 against bitter rivals Leeds was well worth waiting for. Full-back Gerry Byrne played on despite breaking his collarbone in the tenth minute, even managing to set up Roger Hunt who scored the winner in extra-time to make it 2-1!

Wins against Newcastle in 1974, Everton in 1986 and 1989, Sunderland in 1992 and Arsenal in 2001 – the very first time the Cup Final was played at Cardiff 's Millennium Stadium – almost complete the Reds' FA Cup story to date.

But in 2006 Liverpool beat West Ham on penal-ties in one of the most exciting finals for many years, Steven Gerrard scoring twice and turning the match around. The other Reds goal in a 3-3 scoreline at 90 minutes was scored by Djibril Cissé, and Gerrard also starred from the penalty spot as Liverpool closed out the match. Liverpool also appeared in the final in 2012, narrowly going down 2-1 to Chelsea.

Fagan

When Joe Fagan became Liverpool manager in July 1983 at the ripe old age of 63 after Bob Paisley's retirement he, like his predecessor, had no previous managerial experience. He had, however, been a boot room fixture since Bill Shankly's arrival and knew the club's workings inside out.

And the first of his two seasons in charge, 1983-1984, saw Liverpool win their fourth successive League Cup and third successive League Championship. Not only that, they brought up a historic treble by winning the European Cup for the fourth time in eight seasons.

Few changes were made to Bob Paisley's squad but the breakthrough of striker Ian Rush, signed from Chester in 1980 and a regular in the reserves, was important to Fagan's success. He also brought in influential Danish midfielder Jan Molby from Ajax.

Fagan's second and final season saw Everton – of all clubs – take the title with four matches to spare. And, while the Reds reached the European Cup Final once again, their intention of retaining their trophy against Italian champions Juventus was rendered meaningless by off-field events at Brussels' Heysel Stadium. It was a sad end to two eventful years.

Fagan was succeeded by striker Kenny Dalglish, who accepted the role of player-manager. He died at the age of 80 in July 2001.

BELOW Joe Fagan (left) pictured in the dug-out at the 1984 European Cup Final

Fairclough

If ever a player deserved the 'supersub' tag it was red-headed striker David Fairclough. Time and again during his debut season of 1975-76, he left the bench to score crucial goals to help the Reds overhaul QPR and claim the First Division title.

Fairclough, born on 5 January 1957, made his debut – as a sub – in a 4-0 away win over Spurs in December 1975 and made five starts and nine substitute showings in all that campaign. But it was as the season drew to its climax that he really made his mark, netting seven goals in the final eight games. This run included both goals in a 2-0 victory over Burnley and another brace in the penultimate game of the season, a 3-0 away win over Manchester City.

His most spectacular effort came in the derby encounter with Everton in early April. Only two minutes remained when he seemingly took on the whole Everton team in a mazy run from the halfway line before planting the ball beyond Dai Davies. Fairclough's most famous intervention, however, was scoring the spectacular late winner against St Etienne in the second leg of the European Cup quarter-final in March 1977.

Supersub did, in fact, make more starts (92) than substitute appearances (61) for the Reds, helping them retain the championship in 1976-77 and win the European Cup in 1978 before being transferred to Swiss club Lucerne in 1983.

home of local team Ipswich Town, but at heart he remained a Red.

Called upon to be a presenter on TV pop show Top Of The Pops, John would leave the viewer with little doubt as to who he supported; a female relative of the family knitted him a red jumper that simply stated 'League Champions' and then underneath listed each and every year the club had lifted the honour. A year later and John would have a new jumper, newly knitted and bearing testament to the latest success of the men from Anfield. It was a simple yet highly effective statement.

Peel's fellow famous fans range from comedians Stan Boardman and Jimmy Tarbuck to pop stars Ian McCulloch (Echo and the Bunnymen) and Ian Broudie (Lightning Seeds). Singer Cilla Black, Craig Charles of Red Dwarf, actor Ricky Tomlinson and DJ Spoony are also numbered among that elite band of celebrity Kopites.

Even the late Pope John Paul II, hiphop artist Dr Dre, film actress Angelina Jolie, musician Elvis Costello and golfer Laura Davies are known Reds.

LEFT The late great
John Peel, DJ

BELOW Comedian
Jimmy Tarbuck

Famous Fans

Many fans take their love of Liverpool FC to extremes, and the late, great DJ John Peel was no exception. Naming his children William Anfield, Alexandra Anfield, Thomas Dalglish and Florence Shankly betrayed John's lifelong love of the club, even though he lived his later years not on Merseyside but in deepest East Anglia. He would often visit Portman Road,

Firmino

Roberto Firmino Barbosa de Oliveira comes from Maceio, a coastal city in Brazil that was also the birthplace of Mario Zagallo, the first man to win the FIFA World Cup as a player and a manager. Born on 2 October 1991 Bobby Firmino initially moved into European football on New Year's Day 2011 with German outfit Hoffenheim. They signed him from Figueirense where he had debuted three weeks after turning 18 having developed at the club in a defensive midfield role rather than the forward role he plays with such panache and intelligence at Anfield.

16 goals in the Bundesliga in 2013-14 included late season strikes at Bayern Munich and Jurgen Klopp's Dortmund as he was awarded the German 'Breakthrough player' award as the league's fourth top scorer. Continued eye-catching form the following season; which climaxed in the Copa America for Brazil, led to a £29m move to Liverpool with whom he made a swift impact, getting on the score-sheet for the first time in a 4-1 win at Manchester City and ending his initial campaign with 11 goals, including strikes in handsome home wins over both Manchester clubs.

Firmino's second season brought a dozen goals but the third brought 12 in the Champions League alone in a goal-laden campaign of 27 strikes, the tally including Champions League highlights against his old club Hoffenheim and a famous win a Manchester City. A first hat-trick (against Arsenal) came in a 16 goal third season during which Mo Salah and Sadio Mane outscored him but there could be no doubt that the Brazil international's intelligent movement was the catalyst for creating much of the space his fellow members of the front three exploited handsomely thanks to Firmino's unselfishness.

BELOW Firmino playing against Chelsea in January 2017

Fowler

Robbie Fowler (born 9 April 1975) grew up an Everton fan and, like his mentor Ian Rush, made the transition from Goodison to Anfield playing staff.

At the age of 18, Fowler impressed during a summer tournament for the England Under-19s and was expected to start the 1993-94 season as a regular for his club. But though he scored all five in a 5-0 drubbing of Fulham and finished the season with 18, he had to wait until the following campaign to link with his idol regularly.

The youngster opened his account with a hat-trick against Arsenal and was the club's top scorer, earning a Coca-Cola Cup winner's medal after a 2-1 win over Bolton.

In 1995-96 Fowler made way for Stan Collymore, but came back to score a staggering 36 goals, second only to Alan Shearer, and made a long-awaited debut for England in Euro '96, coming on as substitute four times.

During 1996-97, his understanding with Collymore failed to click, prompting the latter's departure, but Fowler scored 31 goals in the season. Then injury struck and, with new boss Gérard Houllier preferring Michael Owen and Emile Heskey up front, Robbie joined Leeds United in a £11 million deal in November 2001.

An injury-hit stay ended when he moved in January 2003 to Kevin Keegan's Manchester City, where he remained until a shock return to Anfield in January 2006.

After short spells at Cardiff City and Blackburn Rovers, Fowler signed with North Queensland Fury in February 2009 and, continuing his career down under, moved to Perth Glory in April 2010.

After shorts spells with Cardiff and Blackburn, he forged a career in Australia with North Queensland Fury and Perth Glory. In 2011, he joined Thai side Muangthong United firstly as a player and latterly as a manager where he remained until his retirement in 2012.

He was capped 26 times for England, scoring seven goals, and was included in England's squads for Euro 1996 and 2000, and the 2002 World Cup. He is now a regular television pundit as well as a millionaire property magnate!

ABOVE Robbie Fowler celebrates after scoring the fourth goal for Liverpool during the UEFA Cup Final, 2001

Gerrard

Steven Gerrard collected almost every club medal during 18 years in the first team and in 2006 was awarded an MBE by the Queen. The one piece of silverware that eluded him was the Premier League title, having come so close under Brendan Rodgers, with whom he had a respectful but lukewarm relationship.

He was also one of the greatest captains of England, having played 114 times for his country including leading the team in the last World Cup in Brazil 2014.

He first played for Liverpool in November 1998 and as a box-to-box midfielder, was instrumental in the Reds winning a unique treble in 2001. With the Worthington and FA Cups already in the cabinet, Gerrard was one of the scorers in an unforgettable 5-4 UEFA Cup final triumph over Alaves. It came as no surprise when the man nicknamed the Huyton Hammer was voted PFA Young Player of the Year.

A mixed domestic season fol-

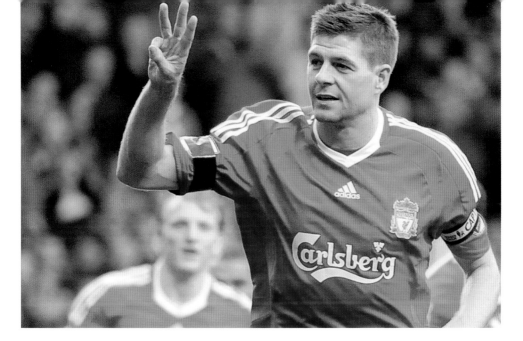

lowed, the highlight of which was a Worthington Cup final at Cardiff's Millennium Stadium. Gerrard opened the scoring in a satisfying 2-0 win over Manchester United.

By the start of 2003-04 the No.8 had firmly established himself as Liverpool's on-field leader, and it was no surprise when Gerard Houllier handed him the captain's armband in place of Sami Hyypia.

Just when it seemed things couldn't get any better for the Scouser, he enjoyed the greatest night of his sport-

ing career. On May 25, 2005, under new boss Rafael Benitez, Gerrard lifted the club's fifth European Cup.

Having already brought Liverpool back from the brink earlier in the campaign with a superlative strike against Olympiacos, the skipper helped inspire the greatest comeback of all time in Istanbul. No one believed the Reds could overturn AC Milan's 3-0 half-time lead - until Stevie G's 54th minute header, that is.

The 2005-06 campaign culminated

ABOVE Steven Gerrard celebrates his third goal against Aston Villa, March 2009

Cup final, and again it was AC Milan. This time, however, the night ended in heartbreak following a 2-1 loss.

Now a bona fide legend of the British game, the midfielder made it a century of club goals with a powerful free-kick against PSV in October 2008. In doing so, he joined an elite band of 16 Anfield legends to achieve the feat.

The strike was one of 24 for Gerrard during 2008-09, a personal record which earned him Football Writers' Player of the Year for the first time. Sadly, his haul wasn't enough to secure an elusive Premier League winners' medal, though Liverpool mounted their best challenge since 1990 before United crossed the line on the penultimate weekend.

A disappointing term followed, though Gerrard still plundered 12 goals as Liverpool finished seventh. He also made his 500th LFC appearance at Ewood Park on December 12, 2009.

In February 2012 he led Liverpool onto the Wembley turf for the first time, and though he missed a penalty in the shoot-out against Cardiff City, it was the Reds who prevailed and Gerrard who climbed the Wembley steps to lift the Carling Cup.

Then, just a few weeks later, he did

with another FA Cup win in Cardiff, with West Ham providing the opposition. If 1953 will always be remembered as the Stanley Matthews final, then 2006 will surely go down as Gerrard's day.

The midfielder twice breached Shaka Hislop's net, including a dramatic equaliser in the dying moments to send the game into extra-time and, ultimately, penalties. This 35-yard volley was voted Match of the Day's Goal of the Season.

In December 2006 the Kop idol was awarded an MBE, which he later collected from the Queen at Buckingham Palace. As if all this wasn't enough, the season ended with another European something, which, even without any of the above, would have made him a legend in the minds of Liverpool fans - he scored a hat-trick in a 3-0 win over Everton at Anfield, a feat that hadn't been achieved since 1935.

In July 2013, Liverpool announced that Gerrard had signed a contract extension with the club, committing his future to the Reds. By finding the net with a penalty against Newcastle at St James' Park in October 2013, Gerrard reached the landmark of 100 goals in the Premier League - only the 12th Liverpool player to achieve such a feat.

In his final season at the club, he made his 500th league appearance in a 0-0 draw against West Brom – becoming only the third ever player to achieve this feat with one club after Ryan Giggs, at Manchester United, and his teammate Jamie Carragher.

In total he played 710 times for Liverpool in all competitions, scoring 186 goals placing him above Robbie 'God' Fowler. His last goal in front of the Kop was a last-minute winning near-post header against QPR after he had missed a penalty earlier in the match. Drama to the last!

He called time on his incredible Anfield career at the end of the 2014-15 season when he went to play at a more leisurely pace for Los Angeles Galaxy – his boots being partly filled by the arrival of James Milner from Man City in July 2015.

After completing his playing days with a couple of years in the MLS with LA Galaxy, Stevie G returned to Liverpool to become coach of Liverpool's under 18s before commencing a career in management with Rangers the following year.

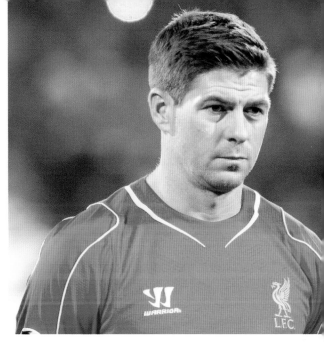

ABOVE Steven Gerrard in 2014

RIGHT A happy Dirk
Kuyt after scoring

BELOW Peter Crouch
shoots to score a goal
for his side

Goals
Goals Goals

Throughout Liverpool's illustrious history, they have been known as an attacking and exciting side with many fantastic individual goal-scorers.

Over the years, a number of players stand out, and a selection of their goal scoring exploits is highlighted here.

Most first team goals Ian Rush	(346)
Most League goals Roger Hunt	(245)
Most FA Cup goals Ian Rush	(39)
Most League Cup goals Ian Rush	(48)
Most European goals Steven Gerrard	(41)
Highest-scoring substitute David Fairclough	(18)
Most hat-tricks Gordon Hodgson	(17)
Most hat-tricks in a season Roger Hunt	(5 in 1961-62)
Most penalties scored Jan Molby	(42)
Most games without scoring Ephraim Longworth	(371)
Youngest goalscorer:	Michael Owen, 17 yrs & 144 days v Wimbledon (a) 6 May 1997
Oldest goalscorer:	Billy Liddell, 38 yrs & 55 days v Stoke City (h) 5 March 1960

Grobbelaar

The shock transfer of Ray Clemence to Spurs at the start of 1981-82 saw a real goalkeeping character hit Anfield – 24-year-old Bruce Grobbelaar, who soon made a name for himself with his clowning antics and spectacular style.

Grobbelaar was born on 6 October 1957 in South Africa. His family later moved to Rhodesia, and the flamboyant youngster soon developed into an all-round sportsman, representing his adopted country at both cricket and baseball at junior level. Football was his first love, however, and he decided to fol-low in his father's footsteps and become a goalkeeper.

Problems with work permits meant that he did not begin his league career in England until he signed for Crewe Alexandra, on loan from Vancouver Whitecaps, in 1979. He then returned to Vancouver and finally signed for Liverpool, for £250,000, in March 1981.

Bruce Grobbelaar never believed in standing around and waiting for shots to come his way. He enjoyed dashing to the edge of his area to catch the ball and surprise advancing forwards, and he managed to surprise quite a few of his own defenders in the process. His goalkeeping was always spectacula

and sometimes suicidal, and he often indulged in bizarre antics during the course of a game. He would run the ball up his back and over his head before clearing, walk on his hands, and engage members of the crowd in conversation. This did not always go down well.

Grobbelaar would doubtless have been forgiven his antics in the early years, had it not been for a number of crucial goal-keeping errors. His habit of charging upfield, his propensity to head the ball out and his dropping of crosses all caused concern. And yet he was clearly an amazingly talented keeper, and he was to play a major part in some remarkably successful Liverpool seasons.

In 1983-84 the Reds won the unique treble of League Championship, League Cup and European Cup. In the Final of the latter competition they faced Roma and, with the game tied at one apiece, the destination of the trophy was to be decided on penalties. Grobbelaar's wobbly legs routine may well have made all the difference: Liverpool won 4-2.

After the Heysel disaster, Grobbelaar considered giving up football. He changed his mind, however, and helped his side to yet more League and Cup success. He remained at Anfield until a move to Southampton in 1994, by which time the Liverpool faithful had well and truly taken him to their hearts.

The later part of Grobbelaar's career was dogged by controversy. He was accused of match-fixing while playing for Liverpool but, after five court hearings of various kinds, was eventually exonerated.

Hamann

Although only at the club for seven years, Dietmar Hamann established himself as an influential midfielder for Liverpool playing in 191 league games and scoring eight goals.

In the 2000–01 season, Hamann won his first big English trophy when Liverpool won a much-celebrated cup treble of the League Cup, FA Cup and UEFA Cup as well as place in the Champions League.

Hamann played a major part in the 2005 Champions League Final win over AC Milan. Although he was suffering a broken toe during the final, his entry as a substitute for Steve Finnan at half time was the catalyst for Liverpool's historic fightback.

The team rallied after being 3–0 down to bring the game back to 3–3 and finally won in the penalty shootout; Hamann also showed a great amount of composure and bravery, as he took and converted the first penalty with his broken foot.

This was not the only key part he played in their Champions league success. Earlier in the tournament Hamann had been forced to stand in for Liverpool's key player Steven Gerrard in the first leg of the last 16 round against Bayer Leverkusen. He excelled in the match and scored a late free-kick as Liverpool won the match 3–1.

Hamann won the FA Cup with Liverpool in May 2006, coming on as a substitute in the second-half. He more than played his part in another trophy win for the Reds, who were 3–2 down to West Ham United at the time he came on.

Steven Gerrard scored an injury-time leveller for Liverpool to take the match to extra-time. Liverpool would go on to win the Cup on penalties after a goalless extra-time. Once again, Hamann scored the first penalty in the shoot-out.

Hamann, who played 59 times for Germany, has also stated that it would be a "dream come true" to manage Liverpool one day.

Hansen

A tall and somewhat skinny defender called Alan Hansen (born on 13 June 1955) came to Anfield from Partick Thistle in 1977. The 22 year-old had cost just £100,000 and, once he had put on a bit of weight, he proved to be the bargain of a lifetime.

It was a while before Hansen became a first-team regular but, from 1981, he teamed up with Mark Lawrenson to form the solid heart of an excellent Liverpool defence. Hansen was a cultured player and, unlike many centre-halves, always looked comfortable on the ball.

He made over 600 appearances for Liverpool, and 26 for Scotland, before injury forced his slightly premature retirement in 1990. Then, although he seemed to be an ideal candidate for management, he decided his destiny lay elsewhere.

Hansen became a television pundit, and was a very entertaining one. Defensive errors frequently incurred his displeasure and, on a Saturday night, many a Premiership footballer must have curled up on the sofa with embarrassment as Hansen got going. He did offer praise from time to time, but he always kept it to a minimum.

Now retired, his greatest television moment came when he declared that United would " never win anything with kids " before they went on to win the league that year.

Heighway

One of comparatively few professional footballers to have a university degree, Steve Heighway was signed by Liverpool from Skelmersdale United in 1970. His plans to become a teacher were abandoned as Heighway, who was born in Dublin on 25 January 1947 and later attended Warwick University, went on to establish himself as one of Liverpool's finest wingers.

Bob Paisley said he was one of the best amateur players he had ever seen. A fixture in the Liverpool side for most of the 1970s, Heighway had great speed as well as an accurate delivery; striker John Toshack frequently benefiting from his pinpoint crosses. He was also a scorer of some tremendous goals, including his side's only strike in the 1971 FA Cup Final against Arsenal. Liverpool lost out on that occasion, but Heighway was soon to collect a chest-full of medals with the Reds.

Between 1970 and 1981, he scored 50 goals in 329 League appearances for Liverpool, but of course he was responsible for many more. During this period he also won 34 caps with the Republic of Ireland team. His playing career almost over, he went to the USA for a while, before returning to Anfield to coach the youth side. He retired from that job in 2007.

Henderson

Captain of the European Champions in 2019 Jordan Henderson is the ultimate team player. In a sport increasingly overtaken by 30 second clips on You Tube and celebrity culture, Henderson is the sort of player who makes any team better but one who rarely gets the credit he deserves.

A grafter who is always in position to receive the ball, making his teammates jobs easier, he is a player who runs tirelessly to cover gaps or when Liverpool are in possession he will take defenders away from the man in possession. Henderson is a footballer with an astute understanding of the game. He reads situations so well and invariably puts the team first.

All this makes him sound like a workhorse, albeit a very good one, but make no mistake about it Jordan is a thoroughbred. His range of passing is superb and while it is infrequently seen as he often occupies a central position his crossing is top class.

Not everyone appreciates how influential Henderson is but manager after manager for both club and country have recognised what he brings to their side. Given a league debut as an 18-year old by Roy Keane at Chelsea for Sunderland in November 2008, Fabio Capello gave Jordan his first cap for England at the age of 20 and 153 days against France at Wembley. Roy Hodgson then awarded

him 26 caps, Sam Allardyce selected him for his solitary game in charge of the national side before Gareth Southgate stepped in and gave him 23 caps up to the semi-final of the Nations Cup in 2019. This took Hendo's total to 51, including the World Cup semi-final in 2018 with him captaining his country on six occasions.

At Liverpool Henderson arrived in the summer of 2011 for a bargain fee reported to be in the range of £16-£20m from Sunderland who he made his Liverpool debut against. Although initially he struggled to make people appreciate what he brought to the side, by the start of the beginning of his fourth season Henderson was appointed vice-captain, skippering the side for the first time in November 2014 before becoming Steven Gerrard's successor the following summer.

Taking over from such a legendary figure was always a tall order but with typical determination and persistence Henderson took the challenge in his stride. As he lifted the Champions League trophy on his 324th appearance for the club no one deserved it more. Let Steven Gerrard be the judge. Writing in 'The Times' he said, "If I had to name someone I regard as the ultimate professional, then Jordan would come right at the top of the list. He is selfless, he puts himself at the back of the queue because he looks after everyone else first. He puts Jordan Henderson last."

Houghton

Fulham manager Malcolm Macdonald rescued Glaswegian midfielder Ray Houghton from the obscurity of West Ham's reserve side and took him to Craven Cottage in 1982. He did well there, becoming a firm favourite with the Fulham fans before Oxford United – at that time in the top division – paid £150,000 to secure his services. A couple of years later, Kenny Dalglish paid more than five times that sum to take him to Anfield.

Houghton, born on 9 January 1962, was a hard-working and skilful player, well practised in the ancient art of dribbling. He spent five years at Liverpool, making around 200 appearances in all and scoring 28 League goals. He was then largely replaced in the side by Steve McManaman and was transferred to Aston Villa before later playing for Crystal Palace, and becoming player-coach at Reading.

Having elected to play for the Republic of Ireland, his father's birthplace, rather than Scotland, Houghton soon established himself as a stalwart of the side. He went on to win a total of 73 caps, mainly while Jack Charlton was in charge, and in 1987, no doubt to the delight of his father and the dismay of his mother, he helped the Republic beat Scotland in a European Championship qualifying game. He is now a media pundit.

BELOW Ray Houghton chases Anton Rogan (left) of Sunderland as Gary Bennett (right) moves in during the FA Cup Final at Wembley, 1992

Houllier/ Hodgson

Appointed as joint manager in July 1998, supplementing existing boss Roy Evans, Gérard Houllier assumed total control four months later.

Born on 3 October 1947, he had begun in management at Le Touquet, followed by spells at Noeux Les Mines, Lens and Paris St Germain. He was assistant manager of the French national side before becoming national coach. An association with Merseyside had begun with a spell as a trainee teacher decades before his second coming.

Houllier's time at Anfield as manager was attended by success, a six-month period from early 2001 seeing the Worthington, FA, UEFA, Community Shield and European Super Cup added to the club's trophy haul. But a game against Leeds United in October 2001 saw him taken ill with heart problems. He resumed the reins from assistant Phil Thompson in March 2002.

He was given two more seasons to add to the 2003 League Cup that was Liverpool's only other honour gained after his extraordinary opening spell, but too many signings proved ineffective and he was replaced by Rafa Benitez in 2004.

Roy Hodgson did not set the world alight as a player, but he arrived at Anfield in July 2010 as one of the most experienced and respected coaches in the world game. His Europe-wide management career has taken in major clubs such as Inter Milan as well as national teams including Finland and Switzerland. The south Londoner returned home in 2007 to take on the challenge of managing Fulham, a task he accomplished with style.

Hodgson looked out of his depth at Liverpool and left after a string of poor results to manage West Bromwich Albion in January 2011. The football world was shocked when he was appointed manager of England over fans' favourite Harry Redknapp – showing its probably easier to manage the national side than the mighty Reds! He went on to become the Premier League's oldest manager with Crystal Palace.

Hughes

Whether it was as skipper of Liverpool or, later as one of TV's Question of Sport captains, you knew what you'd get from Emlyn Hughes: boundless energy and maximum, infectious effort.

Born on 28 August 1947, he was a natural on the big stage, playing 62 times for England, with 23 of those as captain, and was ultimately awarded an OBE for services to the sport.

Signed from Blackpool by Bill Shankly for £65,000 aged only 19, Hughes was nothing if not versatile: he made his Liverpool debut as a left-back in 1967 but he played anywhere at the back or in midfield, where he had much more freedom to attack. He netted his first Reds goal in August 1967 in a 6-0 trouncing of Newcastle, but another key detail from that game was a rugged tackle which, along with his trademark surging runs, earned him the nickname of Crazy Horse.

In 1977 Hughes became the first Liverpool captain to lift the European Cup, as Borussia Moenchengladbach were beaten 3-1, and he repeate

LEFT Crazy Horse enters the pitch, 1975

BELOW Hughes pictured playing for Liverpool in 1970

the feat a year later as Liverpool overcame Bruges 1-0. In all he won five League Championships at Anfield, plus a pair of UEFA Cup winner's medals and an FA Cup winner's medal and, on a personal level, was named the Football Writers' Player of the Year in 1977. After 12 magical seasons at Anfield, Hughes moved to Wolves, leading them to the League Cup in 1980.

Hughes played out his career with Rotherham United (as player-manager), Hull City and Swansea City. Following a high-profile media career and a peaceful retirement, he died in 2004 at the age of 57.

Hunt

Roger Hunt was one of England's heroes in the 1966 World Cup. Born on 20 July 1938 in Golborne, near Warrington, he played initially for Stockton Heath before signing on at Anfield in May 1959. At the time, Liverpool were experiencing life in the relative obscurity of the old Second Division, and were struggling to regain top-flight status.

Phil Taylor brought the aspiring inside-forward to Merseyside, but it was under the inspirational managership of Bill Shankly that Hunt, although never particularly speedy, became one of the best forwards in the country. He was awarded his first England cap during the 1961-62 season, even though he was still not playing at the top.

Hunt scored 21 goals in the 1959-60 season, but his side narrowly failed to win promotion, finishing third behind Aston Villa and Cardiff City. Liverpool came third again in the following year's campaign, but in 1961-62 the Reds finally topped the table. They scored 99 goals in their 42 matches, and Hunt netted 41 of them.

With 'Sir Roger' (as the Kop dubbed him) knocking in the goals, Liverpool were League champions in 1964 and 1966, FA Cup winners and European Cup semi-finalists in 1965, and European Cup Winners Cup runners-up in 1966.

Meanwhile, Hunt's England career blossomed, culminating in his World Cup Final appearance at the expense of Jimmy Greaves. However, no one could say he didn't deserve it, as he had scored three times in the earlier group games. And even though he didn't score in the

BELOW Roger Hunt (second from bottom left) pictured with the Cup-winning 1965 Liverpool team

land, had featured in 34 full international matches, scoring 18 goals. Given his international scoring rate was more than a goal every two games, he probably deserved to have played in more.

Unlike many ex-players, Hunt had no desire to remain in the game when his playing days were over, preferring to work in his family's haulage business. Awarded the MBE in 2000. In later life he ran a joinery business.

ABOVE Roger Hunt evades Norman Hunter of Leeds United in the 1965 FA Cup Final

RIGHT Hunt in action, 1968

Final, his contribution to that memorable occasion was also very significant.

Having scored a remarkable total of 245 goals in 404 League matches, Hunt was rather surprisingly transferred by Shankly to Second Division Bolton Wanderers in 1969. Now 31, he was a little less prolific, but he still managed to score 24 times in 76 League appearances for the Burnden Park club, before calling it a day. By the time he retired in 1973, the modest Roger Hunt, who claimed that he would have scored far fewer goals had he not played alongside some of the best players in the

Hyypia

Arriving at Anfield in 1999 from Dutch side Willem II, centre-back Sami Hyypia (born 7 October 1973) was an instant success, and outlasted more famous fellow Finn Jari Litmanen to play a role in nine seasons of Liverpool football while running up a total of 445 first-team appearances.

He led the team when they won five trophies in 2001 (European Super Cup, Community Shield, UEFA Cup and the two domestic cups), and by the time he left Anfield in the summer of 2009, he had played for Liverpool 317 times and scored 22 goals.

Hyypia played every Champions League game during 2004-05, while his goal against Juventus in the quarter-final first leg did much to keep Liverpool on track for Champions League glory.

While he's a six-footer who is dominant in the air, Hyypia (who began his career in Finland with MYPA-47 before moving to Holland in 1995) is very confident on the ground for such a big man. He is also temperamentally sound, having got through the 2000-01 campaign without incurring a single yellow card

LEFT Hyypia controls the ball for Liverpool

– a remarkable feat for a defender who had played nearly sixty games.

With the arrival of young centre-halves Daniel Agger and Martin Skrtel, it became obvious that Hyypia was approaching the end of his Liverpool career, and he announced that the 2008-09 season would be his last at Anfield after agreeing a two-year deal with German side Bayer Leverkusen. Since retiring from playing in Germany he has gone in to management and had a brief spell in charge of South coast championship side Brighton.

Internationals

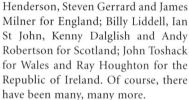

Liverpool Football Club has provided a host of international players down the years – enough to fill a whole book. The first was Harry Bradshaw, who played for England in a 6-0 drubbing of Ireland in 1897. Many more followed, including Rab Howell, also in the late 1890s, who is thought to be the only true Romany to have donned an England shirt.

Since then, an awful lot of famous names have worn the shirts of the home countries, including Roger Hunt, Ray Clemence, Emlyn Hughes, Kevin Keegan, Peter Beardsley, Michael Owen, David James, Jordan Henderson, Steven Gerrard and James Milner for England; Billy Liddell, Ian St John, Kenny Dalglish and Andy Robertson for Scotland; John Toshack for Wales and Ray Houghton for the Republic of Ireland. Of course, there have been many, many more.

With the Premiership now regarded as the most competitive league in the world, many internationals have come to Britain to ply their trade. In the Premier League era, as a leading side Liverpool have attracted top stars from around the globe. For instance, the starting line-up

at the 2019 Champions League final included three Brazilian and two Dutch internationals as well as international stars from Cameroon, Senegal and Egypt along with two Englishman and a Scot, while on the bench were inter-nationals from Belgium, Croatia, Spain and Switzerland. Liverpool's teams orig-inally drew from the 'Home Countries' (England, Scotland, Wales and Northern Ireland) plus Eire. We reproduce here the top five players to have represented these 'traditional' countries while with Liverpool, with the exception of Northern Ireland which has, for some reason, been poorly represented.

TOP FIVES

Number of caps won while with Liverpool (Total number of caps in brackets)

ENGLAND

Caps	Player
114	Steven Gerrard (114)
60	Michael Owen (89)
59	Emlyn Hughes (62)
56	Ray Clemence (61)
50	Phil Neal (50) /
50	Jordan Henderson* (51)

Henderson to start of 2019-20.

SCOTLAND

Caps	Players
55	Kenny Dalglish (102)
37	Graeme Souness (54)
29	Billy Liddell (29)
27	Steve Nicol (27)
26	Alan Hansen (26)

WALES

Caps	Player
67	Ian Rush (73)
26	John Toshack (40)
23	Joe Allen (42)
18	Joey Jones (72)
17	Craig Bellamy (78)

NORTHERN IRELAND

Caps	Player
27	Elisha Scott (31)
12	Billy Lacey (23)
3	David McMullan (3)
2	Ryan McLaughlin (2)

Only four players have been capped with Northern Ireland while with Liverpool

REPUBLIC OF IRELAND

Caps	Player
51	Ronnie Whelan (53)
38	Steve Staunton (102)
34	Ray Houghton (73)
34	Steve Heighway (34)
28	Steve Finnan (53)

ABOVE Elisha Scott in his playing days for Northern Ireland

BELOW Scotland's Kenny Dalglish in action

Johnson

Glen Johnson had already established himself as one of the Premier League's top full-backs in the years prior to his big-money move to Merseyside in June 2009 as well as being an integral part of the national team.

His career began in earnest when he became the first signing for new Chelsea owner Roman Abramovich in 2003. Ironically the Londoner's league debut for the Blues arrived at Anfield in August of the same year. Three months later came an international bow against Denmark as a substitute for Gary Neville.

Johnson won the Premier League and League Cup during his time at Stamford Bridge but was loaned by Jose Mourinho to Portsmouth in 2006 and, after signing, helped the club to FA Cup glory two years later.

A summer move to Merseyside followed, with his debut arriving at White Hart Lane on August 16, 2009. Three days later came Johnson's first goal, an acrobatic volley in a 4-0 thrashing of Stoke.

Injuries punctuated the 2010-11 season but Johnson's form - both on the left and right of defence - following the return of Kenny Dalglish proved to any remaining doubters that both the attacking and defensive sides of his game were top drawer.

In February 2012, his consistency was rewarded with a first medal for the club. Having started the Carling Cup final against Cardiff at Wembley, Johnson kept his nerve to score from 12 yards as Liverpool clinched a shoot-out win.

Under Brendan Rodgers, the defender continued to provide reliable and consistent performances eventually reaching a total of 160 league appearances for the club before completing his playing days at Stoke. Glen was capped 54 times by England.

Johnston

Craig Johnston was an enthusiastic, if unconventional footballer. Born in Johannesburg on 8 December 1960, but brought up in Australia, he joined Liverpool from Middlesbrough for a £650,000 fee in 1981. He seemed to get on all right with Bob Paisley, the manager who signed him, but he was something of a rebel and there was to be frequent conflict with Joe Fagan when the latter took over from Paisley.

Midfielder Johnston, nicknamed 'The Headless Chicken' by Paisley, had a tremendous amount of energy, and it seemed he did not burn it all up on the football field. There were frequent rows and arguments and in 1984, having been taken off during the League Cup Final, he walked out before being presented to the Queen. Whether or not Her Majesty was amused, or whether indeed she noticed, is not recorded.

Johnston suffered from a loss of confidence during his time at Anfield, but this returned when Kenny Dalglish took over as manager. Nevertheless, the headless chicken decided to cluck off at the age of 27, having made 190 League appearances for Liverpool, with 30 goals to his credit. He returned to Australia to care for his invalid sister and develop the Predator football boot.

ABOVE Craig Johnston scores for Liverpool in the 1986 FA Cup Final

Kay

Born in 1891, George Kay was West Ham's captain in the famous White Horse Cup Final of 1923 and had previously been the first Englishman to captain an Irish League club while at Belfast Celtic. Just as his playing career

was affected by World War I, Kay's managerial prowess was interrupted by its successor.

After a five-year stint with Southampton, Kay became Liverpool boss in 1936; his first job was to steer the Reds away from the relegation places. He not only succeeded but also went on to be an outstanding manager, one of his pre-war signings being a certain 17-year-old called Billy Liddell. Later signings included Bob Paisley, from Bishop Auckland, and Albert Stubbins – the latter from under the noses of Everton.

When football resumed after the hostilities, the deep-thinking Kay masterminded a Reds tour of the USA that helped to foster team spirit.

A fit and confident Liverpool started the 1946-47 season in style and went on to take the League championship. Kay also guided Liverpool to the 1950 FA Cup Final, won by Arsenal 2-0, but by then he was struggling with his health and in January 1951 he stood down on doctor's orders. He died a premature death in 1965; after which the great Billy Liddell said: "If any man gave his life for a club, George Kay did so for Liverpool."

Keegan

Joseph Kevin Keegan was born on 14 February 1951 in Armthorpe, near Doncaster. Originally simply a promising young midfielder, he scored 18 goals in 124 League appearances for Scunthorpe United, before being signed by Bill Shankly for a paltry £35,000 in May 1971.

Shankly converted his new signing into an out-and-out striker, and for the next few seasons Keegan and John Toshack formed a formidable attacking duo. Keegan turned out to be one of the most exciting players ever to grace the Anfield arena, and it was not long before he achieved pop-star status, even though his song 'Head Over Heels in Love' barely scraped into the Top 40 in 1979.

Keegan made his England debut in 1972, and went on to play for his country on another 62 occasions, scoring 21 goals. For several years, he was a key member of the side. On the home front, he scored more than 200 goals in a Liverpool shirt before, to everyone's surprise, he opted to move to SV Hamburg for a half-million-pound fee in 1977.

ABOVE Keegan goes in for a tackle

Liverpool's loss was Hamburg's gain, as Keegan went on to be voted European Player of the Year on two occasions.

He again surprised the world of football when he returned to England to play for Southampton in 1980. With another 37 goals in league games to his credit, he then moved to Newcastle United, where he scored another 48 times in 78 League encounters. By now a Newcastle legend, as well as an Anfield hero, in 1984 he quit in favour of a Spanish golf course. Nevertheless, he took over as manager at St James' Park in 1992, then shocked Newcastle by resigning in 1997.

Football had not, however, seen the last of Kevin Keegan. He returned to the game as manager of a resurgent Fulham, and was then appointed to

the top job: manager of the England side, early in 1999. The appointment promised much, but Keegan himself felt he was not quite up to it. Following a 1-0 defeat by Germany in a World Cup qualifying game in October 2000, he resigned in dramatic fashion. His record of played eighteen, won seven, drawn seven,

lost four was actually not very impressive.

Following a spell as manager of Manchester City, a post from which he resigned in March 2005, it was a surprise to most people when he returned to Newcastle United as manager in January 2008. Having signed a contract that would see him through until 2011, Keegan quit Newcastle United after just eight months following a continuing disagreement with the board over the management of the club. A tribunal later ruled that he had been constructively dismissed.

Kennedys

The combined talents of Ray and Alan Kennedy ensured their shared surname remained on Liverpool's team sheet from 1974 to 1985. Unrelated north-easterners, they each played a major role in the club's success as well as representing England. They also combined on the field in memorable fashion to win the 1981 European Cup.

Midfielder Ray, born 28 July 1951, had already achieved the Double with Arsenal in 1970-71 when he became Bill Shankly's last signing at Anfield. His form had been in the doldrums for some time before new boss Bob Paisley switched him from attack to midfield and his confidence was restored.

Liverpool won the League title in 1975-76 and he went on to play a major part in the successes to come. Three European Cup winners' medals, one UEFA Cup, four further Championship

titles and one League Cup were won, along with 17 caps for England in a prolific period for Liverpool as the midfield of Souness, Case, McDermott and Kennedy swept aside all before them.

In 1982, he transferred to John Toshack's Swansea, but things did not work out and he left for Hartlepool before trying his hand at management abroad. In 1985, Ray Kennedy was diagnosed as suffering from Parkinson's Disease and has since spent his time raising public awareness of the illness and dealing with his own health and personal problems.

Alan Kennedy (born 31 August 1954) was an attacking full-back who joined

LEFT Ray Kennedy closes down Gerry Francis of QPR

BELOW In it goes! Ray Kennedy salutes Kenny Dalglish's winning goal as Liverpool win the European Cup in 1978

was everyone's favourite sidekick and regularly bailed the Reds out of trouble with his well-timed interventions. In 1985, however, 31-year-old Kennedy was replaced in the Liverpool side by Jim Beglin and left for his home-town club of Sunderland.

With Liverpool he had won every major honour, except the FA Cup, more than once. He was a tough-tackling defender, but when the time came to counter-attack he had the pace and eye for an opening that proved invaluable.

from first club Newcastle in 1978. He will be remembered for his goal against Real Madrid that won the European Cup Final in Paris in 1981. With the game poised at 1-1 and with just six minutes remaining, Alan ran into Ray's throw and smashed the ball past keeper Agustin.

Three years later in the same competition, he secured the Treble for Liverpool with the decisive penalty in a shoot-out with Roma in Rome. The capture of the European Cup, League Championship and League Cup led to Kennedy being selected for England by Bobby Robson that summer.

He was lauded by the Kop, who nicknamed him Barney Rubble because he

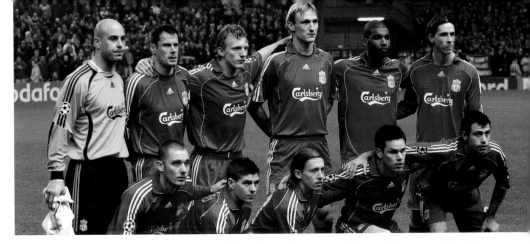

Kit

Prior to the Bill Shankly era, Liverpool had worn red shirts and white shorts since their original blue and white quarters were discarded in the 1898 season. But just as Leeds rival Don Revie boosted his side's fortunes by adopting Real Madrid's all-white, so Shankly hit upon the idea of wearing all red.

It's said that the decision was made after Liverpool were drawn against Anderlecht in the second round of the club's first European Cup campaign in 1964-1965. Captain Ron Yeats, said Shankly, would look even bigger if he wore red shorts, while Ian St John suggested red socks to complete the now-legendary all-red kit.

There have been several cosmetic tweaks over the years, most notably the yellow pinstripes of the mid-1980s and the Adidas 'three stripe' adornments that followed, while the liver bird badge with the LFC letters below it came off the white oval background to be embroidered directly on the shirt. It was then surrounded by a shield.

Away kits have varied from green through white to grey, and, like the home kit, have been dominated by sponsors' logos. Yet these have been mercifully few. While the 1980s saw Crown Paints splashed on red shirts, Carlsberg were the club's sponsors from 1992 until 2010, in the longest partnership in world football. Shirts now bear the name of the Standard Chartered bank.

Klopp

FAR RIGHT Jurgen
Klopp - Liverpool's first
German manager

To be in the company of Bob Paisley, Joe Fagan and Rafael Benitez, Jurgen Klopp is part of an exceptional group as a manager who brought Europe's Premier trophy to Anfield. Worthy winners of the Champions League in 2019, Klopp had inspired his team on to greater glory after the disappointment of being beaten finalists a year earlier.

Like many successful managers Klopp had a lengthy but not noteworthy playing career. He spent over a decade with Mainz 05 eventually becoming their manager in February 2001. His achievements from the dug-out quickly began to outshine his playing days when effort and enthusiasm endeared him to supporters much more than his limited quality on the ball was able to.

Once in charge of dictating playing style Jurgen introduced the pressing style which has become his trademark. Transforming the team he inherited from strugglers to challengers got Klopp noticed, especially when he led his club to a first ever promotion to the Bundesliga in 2004 followed by European qualification. While the bub-ble burst with relegation Jurgen's loyalty saw him remain before an eventual resignation after an unsuccessful season trying to regain their top-flight place. In total the Stuttgart born boss had devoted 18 years of his life to the club.

His achievements had caught the attention of Borussia Dortmund who appointed him in 2008 as he left Mainz. Despite competition in the shape primarily of Bayern Munich, under Klopp Dortmund won the Bundesliga in 2011 and managed to retain their title as Jurgen won successive Manager of the Year awards. Dortmund also took the domestic cup the DFB Pokal as well as the Bundesliga in 2012.

In 2012-13 Klopp took Dortmund to the final of the Champions League, losing an all-German final to Bayern after defeating Real Madrid in the semi-final. There was some consolation in Dortmund taking the German Supercup in 2013 and again a year later.

Leaving Dortmund in the summer of 2015 after again reaching the final of the DFB Pokal Jurgen arrived at Anfield on 8 October 2015, taking over from Brendan Rodgers. Oddly his first game was against Spurs – the side who he would be opponents on the day

72 | THE BEST OF LIVERPOOL

he joined the ranks of Champions League / European Cup winning managers at Liverpool.

There were two cup finals in Klopp's first season on Merseyside although defeat in the League Cup and Europa League finals to Manchester City and Seville were disappointments, the former on penalties.

Manchester City would be handsomely defeated 5-1 on aggregate in the Champions League quarter-final in 2018 en-route to a final which brought defeat at the hands of Real Madrid but 12 months later came triumph as Jurgen took a team to the Champions League final for the third time in seven seasons. Having steered the Reds to a sensational semi-final victory over Barcelona Klopp masterminded victory over Tottenham in Madrid as he went on to be named Onze d'Or Coach of the Year.

Liverpool fans had taken Klopp to their hearts long before he delivered the trophy of trophies. His passion and ability to motivate and inspire all around him make him the ideal fit for Anfield.

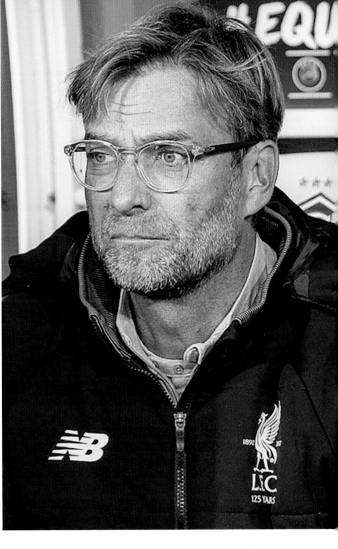

Kop

The banked terrace behind the goal was first named the Spion Kop in 1906 after the site of a battle in the Second Boer War where British forces suffered particularly heavy losses (kop is Afrikaans for hill).

At its height, the Kop was one of the largest single-tier football stands in the world and could hold 28,000 spectators, but the Taylor Report that followed the tragedy at Hillsborough meant that the days of watching top-class football from standing terraces were numbered.

So it was inevitable that a tear would be shed as the bulldozers moved in to prepare the Kop for all-seater status after the home game against Norwich on 30 April 1994. Yet with so many Liverpool families having suffered tragic loss at Hillsborough, no one needed telling that it had to be done. By the time it had

been completely rebuilt as an all-seater stand in 1994, the Kop's capacity had shrunk to 12,409.

Legend has it that the fans could suck the ball into the goal if Liverpool were playing towards that end. Many other grounds boast a kop, but this is the original and best with a capital K.

Kuyt

Renowned more at Anfield for his self-less running and work rate than for a spectacular strike record, Dirk Kuyt still weighed in with some vital goals in his six seasons with Liverpool.

Born on 22 July 1980, Kuyt arrived in the summer of 2006 having established himself as one of Holland's best strikers, with 83 goals in 122 appearances during three seasons with Feyenoord.

He had been utilised more as a winger at his previous club, FC Utrecht, a role manager Rafael Benitez seemed to prefer for him in the Premiership.

Although often playing out wide, he scored in his first ever Champions League Final for Liverpool against AC Milan having scored a goal in the quarter-final against Arsenal and in the semi-final against Chelsea.

He will always have a place in the hearts of the fans for scoring two penalties in a derby against Everton as well as his first hat-trick for Liverpool against Manchester United in March 2011.

His extra time goal at Wembley when he came on as a substitute against Cardiff City in the 2012 League Cup Final helped win the trophy for the club – surprisingly his only trophy as a Liverpool player.

After more than 200 appearances, and some 50 goals, for the Reds he joined Fenerbahce in June 2012. A top player who was often somewhat under-rated, he also made 104 appearances for the Netherlands before retiring from international football in December 2014. In April 2015, Kuyt's career came full circle when he signed a one-year contract to rejoin his former club Feyenoord.

Lawler

ABOVE Chris Lawler pictured in 1970

Bill Shankly inherited a side that needed a stronger and more effective defence, and for this reason Chris Lawler was to become a key member of his side.

Born in Liverpool on 20 October 1943, Lawler's first ambition was fulfilled when he signed for his hometown club as a 17-year-old. Strong and very quick moving for a six-footer, Lawler occupied the right-back position with distinction for many years. His turn of speed meant that he was capable of running down the flank and crossing the ball for others to score, although in his 406 league appearances for Liverpool he netted himself on 41 occasions.

Lawler played just four times for England, but had the gods been on his side he might have featured in many more internationals. As it was, he gave sterling service to his chosen club before moving to Portsmouth to play under former colleague Ian St John in 1975. At Fratton Park he made a further 36 league appearances before ending his playing career at Stockport County – where he scored three times in another 36 games.

Later, a testimonial match was held for him at Anfield, which was attended by 20,000 loyal Liverpudlians.

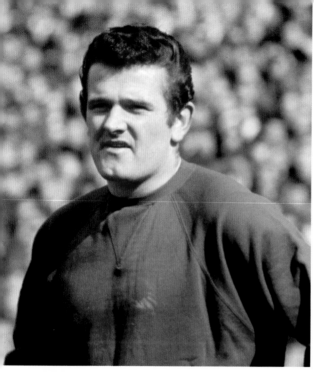

Lawrence

Ayrshire-born Tommy Lawrence moved south with his parents to Warrington before becoming one of the many Scottish footballers to earn fame and modest fortune with Bill Shankly's Liverpool.

Born on 14 May 1940, he showed promise as an amateur goalkeeper before going to Anfield for a trial. He signed professional at 17 and spent the next few years playing junior and reserve team football, finally making his League debut in 1962.

Lawrence measured 5ft 11in and presented a somewhat stocky appearance, but this did not prevent him from becoming an excellent custodian. Liverpool fans affectionately called him the Flying Pig and, rather like his Anfield descendant Bruce Grobbelaar, he became famous for racing out of his area to hoof the ball upfield. Given that the Liverpool defence was so accomplished at the time, this may well have arisen from boredom.

During his seven-and-a-half seasons of first-team football with Liverpool, Lawrence missed just five games, but he earned a mere three caps for Scotland – a country not generally noted for the excellence of its goalkeepers.

Lawrence was exceptionally loyal to his club and did not really want to move to Tranmere Rovers when his transfer was arranged in 1971. He ended his playing days at non-league Chorley in 1973, after which he worked at a wire factory in Warrington. A much loved player, Tommy Lawrence passed away in 2018, aged 77.

Lawrenson

Mark Lawrenson, born in Preston on 2 June 1957, played for North End, and then Brighton, but in his early years his abilities as a defender hardly set the football world alight. He was, however, targeted by Bob Paisley and, in 1981, moved to Liverpool for a surprisingly large £900,000 fee.

As ever, Paisley knew what he was doing. Lawrenson was dogged by injury in his later years, but between 1981 and 1986 his pace, timing and overall footballing intelligence meant that he contributed in no small measure towards the frequent lifting of silverware at Anfield.

Lawrenson won 38 caps for his chosen country, the Republic of Ireland, but many in England wished he had chosen the Three Lions instead. His mum, who collected every article and programme in which his name appeared, would perhaps have been even more proud of her son.

When Achilles tendon trouble ended his playing days, Lawrenson embarked upon a managerial career, but it proved less than successful. He was at Oxford and Peterborough United before moving to Newcastle as defensive coach (a job nobody envied). He is now a noted pundit on radio and television, where his Achilles tendon is safe from further injury unless Gary Lineker gives him a surreptitious kick under the table.

LEFT Mark Lawrenson on the ball

BELOW Lawrenson heads the ball during the European Cup Final against Roma, 1984

BELOW The victorious
Liverpool team that
won the League Cup
in 1984

League Cup

The Football League Cup, otherwise known as Hardaker's Folly after the man whose vision it was, could never have been termed a runaway success. Indeed, Liverpool and Everton initially declined the invitation to enter, in common with other leading clubs, considering it less as a potential crowd-puller, more as unwanted extra fixtures.

The introduction of a one-legged

Wembley final and a place in Europe for the winner changed all that, and it was this that brought the first meeting of Merseyside's top two teams on the north London hallowed turf. Even the first Charity Shield the pair had contested, in 1966, had been played at Goodison.

The League Cup Final of 1984 was the match Merseyside had waited nearly a century for ... but the result in the pouring rain was an anti-climactic scoreless draw. The lack of goals was probably not surprising, since the teams boasted two of the meanest defences in the League. No one wanted to lose this game, so the result was perhaps the best one. And the combined chants of 'Merseyside' that rose from the terraces confirmed that this had been no ordinary fixture, these were no ordinary supporters.

The replay was staged four days later at Maine Road, 52,089 Merseysiders making the pilgrimage down the East Lancs Road. Maybe coats could have been put down in Stanley Park ...

It was always likely that one goal would be enough to decide things, and it was an undistinguished Graeme Souness effort that skidded past Neville Southall that settled the destination of the silverware.

The Reds' first visit to a League Cup Final six years earlier had ended in replay defeat to Brian Clough's Nottingham Forest, but the Everton fixture was their fourth final in succession. West Ham, Spurs and Manchester United were the victims in an unparalleled 'four in a row'. All four games, interestingly, went to extra time, while dispatching West Ham had required a Villa Park replay after a 1-1 Wembley draw.

The Reds' 1987 visit to Wembley saw them lose 2-1 to Arsenal, but normal service was resumed in 1995 as Bolton were dispatched by a Steve McManaman brace. There followed three visits to the Millennium Stadium, Cardiff, a win on penalties against Birmingham City in 2001 followed by a record seventh win in 2003 against Manchester United and defeat to Chelsea in 2005. Liverpool recently won the Carling Cup (now known as the Capital One Cup) in 2012 when they beat Cardiff on penalties after drawing 2-2 at the end of full time. It was the last trophy for the team under the managership

of King Kenny.

No one has won the League Cup as many times as Liverpool who came within a penalty shoot-out of adding a ninth success in 2016 when following a 1-1 draw with Manchester City at Wembley the Reds succumbed 3-1 on spot-kicks.

ABOVE Alan Hansen and Kenny Dalglish hold the trophy after their victory in the League Cup Final against West Ham, 1981

BELOW Liverpool have a champagne party to celebrate clinching the League Cup against Birmingham City, 2001

Lest We Forget

Two tragedies in 1985 and 1989 will forever be remembered not only by Liverpool supporters but by football as a whole.

On 29 May 1985, when England, and much of Europe, was in the grip of so-called 'football hooliganism', Liverpool were playing in the European Cup Final against Juventus. The venue was the Heysel Stadium in Brussels, a crumbling edifice that was palpably unsuitable for the purpose, and had in fact been condemned as a venue for major matches.

Liverpool had objected that a neutral section of the ground set aside for Belgian fans would lead to both sets of supporters buying tickets from touts, and such warnings proved well-founded as this area filled with Italian fans.

Fighting broke out during the game, a wall collapsed and carnage resulted. As the Liverpool website states, "Instead of leaving Brussels having seen our team lift a fifth European Cup, Liverpool supporters travelled back to England having witnessed the deaths of 38 Italians and one Belgian." English teams were immediately banned from European competition for six years.

When Liverpool and Juventus were drawn together in the Champions League in 2005, their first meeting since the Heysel tragedy, many former players and some supporters attempted to heal the wounds with symbolic ceremonies and acts of friendship.

At Hillsborough, Sheffield on 15 April 1989, 96 Liverpool fans waiting to watch their side contest an FA Cup semi-final against Nottingham Forest were to lose their lives. The tragedy threw any event on

ABOVE The Liverpool team stand for a minute's silence for the victims of the Hillsborough disaster

the pitch into perspective and made a mockery of the saying attributed to Bill Shankly that "football's not a matter of life and death … it's more important than that."

Once again, the event was witnessed by millions via their television screens. On this occasion, it was Liverpool supporters who were suffocated or crushed to death, when the police allowed too many people to enter the Leppings Lane end of the ground. Even before the game kicked off, it was clear to many that there was severe overcrowding at one end of the stadium, but still the fans piled in.

By the time the referee abandoned the game after just six minutes, people were climbing over the barriers and onto the pitch in an effort to escape being crushed. Some of them made it. Ninety-five did not (one fan survived and died later).

It was a disaster of unparalleled proportions, and it would lead to revolutionary changes at football grounds throughout the country.

The dead of Hillsborough are commemorated by a memorial next to the Shankly Gates at Anfield. Its eternal flame signifies that their memory will live for ever. Sheffield Wednesday, after years of lobbying by relatives, erected a memorial at the site of the tragedy in 1999.

In 2019 Ch Supt David Duckenfield stood trial for the gross negligence manslaughter of 95 supporters (There could be no prosecution for Tony Bland who passed away in 1993 following brain damage). The jury failed to reach a verdict on a charge Mr Duckenfield denied. The Crown Prosecution Service were quoted as saying they would seek a re-trial. Graham Mackrell, the former Sheffield Wednesday club secretary was found guilty of a health and safety charge.

Liddell

If you are a superstar at Liverpool in the modern era you join a team of superstars. In Billy Liddell's era Liverpool were not the European powerhouse they have been for over four decades. Liddell though was such a star and so synonymous with the club that people referred to 'Liddellpool'. Had he been able to be cloned Billy could have filled the team as

he played in all 10 outfield positions for the club although his main position was on the left wing.

These days, Billy Liddell perhaps appears to be something of an unsung hero, although older Liverpool supporters will remember the 'Flying Scotsman' with deep affection. Born in Dunfermline on 10 January 1922, he was a speedy left-winger with a remarkable appetite for scoring goals.

Although Liverpool won the League championship in 1947 and reached the FA Cup Final in 1950, Liddell's side was mainly a Second Division outfit during his time at Anfield. Honours were therefore few and far between.

It was the duty of the old-fashioned winger to make goals for others. This Liddell duly did but, in his 495 Liverpool league games, he scored a remarkable 216 goals himself. Between 1946 and 1958, he averaged 38 League games per season. He also played 29 times for Scotland, scoring eight times including one in a famous win over England at Wembley in 1951.

'King Billy' was one of football's gentlemen. He seldom committed a foul and showed true remorse when he occasionally did. He played until he was 38, but in the days when footballers were paid nothing like today's inflated wages, he prepared himself for life after football: while still playing, he qualified as an accountant. Billy Liddell died, aged 78, in 2001.

Billy's international experience also included scoring with a header against England in a 5-4 war-time (therefore unofficial) international at Hampden Park. As well as representing the Football League, The F.A., The R.A.F. and the Scottish Services XI most importantly Liddell joined Stan Matthews in being one of only two men selected to play for Great Britain twice. In 1947 a crowd of 137,000 saw Billy play in a 6-1 victory over the Rest of Europe while eight years later he played in a game to mark the Irish FA's 75th anniversary, on that occasion the continentals winning 4-1.

Liddell played on for Liverpool until 1961, his farewell appearance against Southampton at the age of 38 and 224 days making him the club's oldest player, a record that stood until 1990 when surpassed by his fellow Scot Kenny Dalglish.

Billy had joined Liverpool before World War Two but had to wait until the resumption of football after the war to make his official debut – alongside Bob Paisley who he enjoyed an excellent understanding with. Like Paisley, Liddell

is a true Liverpool legend.

'King Billy' was one of football's gentlemen. He seldom committed a foul and showed true remorse when he occasionally did. Although he played until his late thirties he never made a lot of money from a game that nowadays provides untold riches for any player able to play regularly at top level. He turned down the opportunity to line his pockets by rejecting the opportunity to join several other stars of the day in moving to Columbia in 1950 at a time when the maximum wage in England was £12 a week (and £10 during the summer). As Columbia was outside FIFA jurisdiction they were able to offer mega-money for the day and tempted some big names. Liddell stayed with Liverpool through a combination of club loyalty and the recent arrival of twins.

Eventually having given over two decades of service Liddell enjoyed a Testimonial at Anfield, an adoring attendance of just under 39,000 belatedly ensuring Billy enjoyed some financial reward for his loyalty and one of the most significant contributions anyone has ever made to the club.

Billy Liddell passed away, aged 78, in 2001.

Lloyd

The 20-year-old Larry Lloyd made the move north from Bristol Rovers to Liverpool in April 1969. Bought by Bill Shankly to take over from the mighty Ron Yeats, Lloyd didn't disappoint. Like big Ron, the incoming centre-half was from the old school of defending, commanding in the air and strong in the tackle.

He made his first team debut at Dundalk in the old Fairs Cup in September 1969 and was selected for eight League games that season as he was eased into the Anfield set-up.

Lloyd missed only a couple of League games the following season and chalked up an FA Cup Final appearance, only for Arsenal to win the contest in extra time. After a close run for the League title in 1971-72 Lloyd enjoyed his best season for Liverpool the following year, being ever present as the Reds pulled off a memorable League and UEFA Cup double. In fact, he topped off the European campaign by scoring the all-important third goal in the first leg against Borussia Moenchengladbach. The Germans pulled two goals back in the return match, but Liverpool held on.

In August 1974 he moved on to Coventry City, but it was Brian Clough who relaunched his career by taking him to Nottingham Forest in 1976. There he won another League title and two European Cup winners' medals plus two League Cup winners' medals.

After a period as a radio pundit, Lloyd is now involved in management in Spain.

Lucas

The South American holding midfielder Lucas Leiva found it tough to win over fans during the initial stages of his Anfield career but his class shone through so that he is now a regular name on the back of supporters' shirts.

His arrival from Brazil in 2007 was seen as quite a coup for Rafael Benitez, with a host of European clubs apparently circling, and he notched up more than 30 appearances in his debut season, breaking his Anfield duck in style with a 25-yard curler in the FA Cup against Havant and Waterlooville.

The No.21 played a further 39 appearances during his second season at Anfield despite stiff competition from established stars Mascherano and Xabi Alonso. The highlight came when he stood in for the latter as Liverpool thrashed title rivals Manchester United 4-1 at Old Trafford in March 2009.

The Brazilian was voted Young Player of the Season for 2009-10 - proof of how far he'd come in the eyes of Kopites - and in the following season, with Kenny Dalglish now at the helm, the likeable midfielder went one better by winning the fans' Player of the Season.

By now one of the first names on the team-sheet for Brazil, his performances just kept getting better in 2011-12 and he was being hailed as one of the Premier League's finest deep midfielders. His campaign ended cruelly in November when he suffered an anterior cruciate ligament injury to his knee during a Carling Cup victory at Stamford Bridge.

Whilst injuries may have blighted his Liverpool career he has still played more than 270 times for the club. He has latterly been joined by Brazilians, Philippe Coutinho, the club's Player of the Year for the 2014-15 season, and Roberto Firmino, who joined for £29m in June 2015.

The diminutive playmaker's sublime passing range and eye for goal have made him a firm favourite amongst Kopites as well as his fellow players, who voted him the only player from Liverpool to make the PFA Team of the Year in 2015.

ABOVE Lucas Leiva

Managers

ABOVE A 1932
Liverpool team photo,
with George Patterson
(bottom row far left)

RIGHT The Liverpool
team pictured in 1905
with manager Tom
Watson (middle row
far right)

1892-96	WE Barclay	1928-36	George Patterson
1896-1915	Tom Watson	1936-51	George Kay
1920-23	David Ashworth	1951-56	Don Welsh
1923-28	Matt McQueen	1956-59	Phil Taylor

1959-74	Bill Shankly
1974-83	Bob Paisley
1983-85	Joe Fagan
1985-91	Kenny Dalglish
1991-94	Graeme Souness
1994-98	Roy Evans
1998-2004	Gerard Houllier
2004-2010	Rafael Benitez
2010-2011	Roy Hodgson
2011-2012	Kenny Dalglish
2012-2015	Brendan Rogers
2015-Present	Jurgen Klopp

LEFT Liverpool manager Kenny Dalglish, pictured with coaches (and future managers) Ronnie Moran and Roy Evans, celebrating becoming League Champions in 1990

BELOW A shot from 1969, which includes five past managers of the club. Roy Evans (back row third from left), Ronnie Moran (2nd row on left) Bob Paisley and Bill Shankly (third row on left) and Joe Fagan (third row second from right)

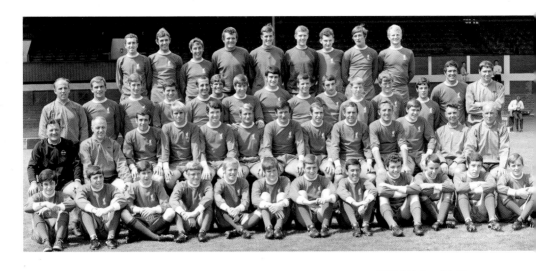

Mane

Top players keep getting better. This has certainly been the case for Sadio Mane at Liverpool. Recognised as a real talent when bought from Southampton in 2016 Sadio showed continued development at Anfield.

By 2018-19 when he was joint Golden Boot winner in the Premier League alongside Mo Salah and Arsenal's Pierre-Emerick Aubameyang with 22 goals, over all competitions Mane managed 26 goals in 50 games. These included two in a Champions League win at Bayern Munich and when international goals are added on Sadio hit the 30 mark for the season.

A year earlier he had 20 goals for Liverpool, a tally that included a hat-trick against Porto and a goal against Real Madrid while in the previous campaign – his first at the club he scored an encouraging 13 – but that was only half his tally as he helped Liverpool become Kings of Europe in 2018-19.

Born in Sedhiou in Senegal, a month before Liverpool lifted the FA Cup in 1992, Sadio progressed through the Senegalese Football Academy, earning a move to Metz in France shortly before his 20th birthday. While Metz were relegated in his few months with the club, scouts had taken notice and eight months after arriving in Europe a reported fee approaching £4m captured him for Red Bull Salzburg. Sadio's second season in Austria brought him the double of league and cup with Red Bull almost tripling their investment on the player when selling him to Southampton that summer.

The scorer of three hat-tricks in Austria, Mane ripped up the record book by registering three goals in two minutes and fifty-six seconds against Aston Villa at the end of his first season – the previous quickest hat-trick in the Premier League scorer having been Robbie Fowler.

Scoring three goals in two games against Liverpool – plus a hat-trick against Manchester City – in his second season at St. Mary's helped persuade Liverpool to pay £34m to bring Mane to Merseyside. Had he maintained his Southampton form he would have been a good signing but Sadio has just kept improving.

McDermott

Terry McDermott served the club well over his eight seasons at Anfield, a period that netted 11 major honours. Those honours included three European Cups, in the first of which he played an important part by scoring a brilliant opening goal in the 3-1 win over Borussia Moenchengladbach in Rome in 1977.

McDermott, born in 8 December 1951 in Kirkby, Merseyside, started his career at Bury before moving on to Newcastle United in 1973 and Liverpool a year later. He was to go on to achieve the rare feat of winning both the Football Writers' and the PFA Player of the Year awards in 1980.

Despite the fact that he was a fine ball-winner and innovative playmaker, McDermott always felt insecure in the team and it was in the 1982-83 season that he returned to Newcastle after an indifferent finale to a glorious career at Anfield. He had played 232 times and scored 54 goals for the Reds.

At St James' Park he became assistant manager to Kevin Keegan as Sir John Hall poured millions into a rebuild-ing programme. He went on to work there as a member of the backroom staff with former Anfield favourites Kenny Dalglish and Graeme Souness as well as Glenn Roeder, Sam Allardyce and Keegan again. He was also capped 25 times for England, and has had an extensive coaching career with Newcastle (twice), Huddersfield Town, Birmingham City and Blackpool.

ABOVE Terry McDermott takes the ball past Trevor Brooking of West Ham United, 1977

McMahon

Former Evertonian Steve McMahon (born 20 August 1961) crossed Stanley Park in a roundabout way via Aston Villa in 1985, having enhanced his reputation as a battling midfielder during his two years in the Midlands. He became Kenny Dalglish's first signing, and the £350,000 was well spent.

Graeme Souness's departure for Italy had left a gap in Liverpool's midfield that had never been properly filled. In McMahon, Dalglish saw a man equally capable of the bone-crunching tackle or defence-splitting pass, someone who could bring bite and subtlety in equal measure, a combination sorely lacking in the existing Liverpool midfield.

Playing in perhaps the last great Liverpool side, McMahon secured League Championship and FA Cup winning medals, not to mention 17 caps for England (he was selected in Bobby Robson's World Cup squad for Italia '90.)

The irony of Mahon's Anfield career is the fact it was curtailed by the very man he was bought to replace – Graeme Souness. After six seasons and more than 200 games at the club, McMahon was shipped out to Manchester City for £900,000; he was sorely missed.

He began a management career in promising style, winning the Second Division championship for Swindon Town after it seemed the Wiltshire club was in freefall, but later efforts with the likes of Blackpool failed to bear fruit and he'd appeared to have settled for life as a media commentator, before heading for Australia and taking over as head coach of Perth Glory in 2005. His tenure was short and McMahon has since resumed his media career.

McManaman

On his debut in December 1990, floppy-maned Steve McManaman (born 11 February 1972) was hailed as a winger with unlimited talent. Born on Merseyside, McManaman's willowy build belied a powerful turn of pace. Though his goalscoring record was disappointing, a spectacular brace against Bolton Wanderers in the 1995 Coca-Cola Cup Final were rated among the finest goals seen at Wembley in recent years.

After an impressive debut season ending in an FA Cup win against Sunderland, McManaman lost his way during the next campaign, but his form at club level returned as he forged a potent partnership with another former apprentice, Robbie Fowler, their burgeoning understanding one of the real plus points of some underachieving seasons.

McManaman's impressive displays saw him claim an England place, making his debut in November 1994, but having established himself as a regular he fell out with then-boss Glenn Hoddle and never had a look-in under Sven

Goran Eriksson.

Made club captain after turning down a move to Barcelona, he had played 364 games (66 goals) in red when he became the first major Liverpool player to leave Anfield on a Bosman free transfer when he joined Real Madrid in the summer of 1999. He scored spectacularly in the European Cup Final against Valencia to end a successful first season at the Bernabeu, but he increasingly found himself marginalised and returned to the Premiership with Kevin Keegan's Manchester City in 2003. Injury blighted his Maine Road stay and he was freed in 2005, age 33.

Retirement has seen McManaman pursue a successful media career in Europe and Asia.

Melwood

Liverpool Football Club's training ground, Melwood, has been used by the club since the 1950s, when it was bought from St Francis Xavier RC school. The name came from two of the priests, Father Melling and Father Woodcock, who taught the boys football.

A wooden pavilion was replaced by a brick one, but little else was done to develop Melwood until January 2001, when the Millennium Pavilion started to take shape. This included a press room, offices for manager and coaches and expanded changing facilities. On the health and fitness side, a gymnasium (split into two areas and computer controlled) is accompanied by a physiotherapy room and small hydrotherapy pool, which can be used in all weathers.

There are several full-size pitches at Melwood, while a small covered area lets play-

ers train on a synthetic surface when the weather is unfavourable.

In the old days security was lax, but nowadays each player has his own key card that allows them entry to the ground. Training schedules vary according to managers' wishes, but morning sessions are often supplemented by evening work. Most players will sign autographs before or after training or pose for a photograph with fans who travel from around the world to see their heroes.

A new £50m training ground at Kirkby, under construction in 2019, will see Liverpool leave their traditional training base for a state of the art new base.

Merseyside Final

The 1980s brought three Cup Final meetings between Liverpool and Everton: the League Cup in 1984 and FA Cup in 1986 and 1989. There were those who wondered why a local contest should have to transport itself 200 miles south to be decided, but half of the city enjoyed taking the day trip to Wembley (and another to Maine Road, after the League Cup Final was drawn).

The first FA Cup Final in '86 was won 3-1 by Liverpool, giving them the League and Cup Double for what was only the third time by any team in the 20th century. Though Gary Lineker opened the scoring, it was man of the match Ian Rush who equalised before setting up Craig Johnston to put the Reds ahead. A second from Rushie rubbed salt in the wound.

A different kind of wound, Hillsborough, overshadowed the second FA Cup meeting in 1989. Some would say the game re-established some sense of normality in a city that had, perhaps, taken the Shankly aphorism about football being more important than life or death too literally until then. The match went into extra time at 1-1, at which point Rush, the hero three years earlier, came off the bench to score two more goals, the first equalised by Stuart McCall, to add to John Aldridge's early strike and establish a winning 3-2 lead.

Some from the blue side of the city resented the fact that somehow they were expected to roll over and let Liverpool win it 'for the fans'. But a hard-fought five-goal thriller was, for the neutral at least, a football showcase and a great advert for the city.

BELOW The team captains Ronnie Whelan and Kevin Ratcliffe of Everton shake hands before the FA Cup Final in 1989

RIGHT Molby controls the ball for Liverpool

BELOW Jan Molby charges with the ball against Newcastle in 1985

Molby

A superb passer and possessor of a lethal shot, Jan Molby started his playing career with his hometown club, Kolding, in Denmark before moving to Ajax Amsterdam.

At the age of 21, the 'Great Dane' was signed by Joe Fagan in August 1984 for £200,000 in the wake of Graeme Souness's departure.

Molby's wonderful range of measured and incisive passing fitted the Liverpool bill perfectly, although his Anfield career was subsequently blighted by weight problems and a spell in prison for a driving offence. If Molby was very handy at free-kicks he was deadly at penalties, netting 40 out of 42 for the Reds and even helping himself to a hat-trick of spot-kicks against Coventry City in the League Cup in November 1986.

In that season, Liverpool claimed the League and FA Cup Double – rivals Everton were runners-up in both competitions – and the Danish international was instrumental in all three FA Cup Final goals as Liverpool recovered from going a goal behind to win 3-1. Prolific goalscorer Ian Rush, in particular, was one of a number of strikers to benefit from Molby's assists.

Further League titles were clinched in 1988 and 1990 and another FA Cup success followed in 1992. Molby was released by Liverpool in February 1996 when he joined Swansea City as player-manager, but was afforded a testimonial for his ten-plus years at Anfield. He then enjoyed a less stellar management career with Kidderminster (twice) and Hull.

Now, like so many former footballers, he is pursuing a career in the media.

Neal

The ever-dependable Phil Neal (born 20 February 1951) had racked up almost 200 appearances for Northampton Town before he became Bob Paisley's first signing in October 1974 and was pitched into the Liverpool way of things immediately with a derby encounter at Goodison Park.

Neal went on to become one of the most decorated footballers in the English game; it's easier to name the one competition – the FA Cup – in which he did not claim a winner's medal than those in which he did. He helped Liverpool to the League championship in his first full season (1975-76), the first of eight such triumphs. League Cup winner's medals were garnered in four successive seasons, while in European competitions Neal and Liverpool were UEFA Cup winners in 1976 and European Cup champions in 1977, 1978, 1981 and 1984.

LEFT Phil Neal is poised to make a pass for Liverpool

Although a midfielder with Northampton, he made the right-back position his own at Anfield – and for England, gaining 50 caps – although he was able to play anywhere along the back four. He took over penalty-taking duties from Kevin Keegan during the 1975-76 season and it was his spot-kick that sealed the club's first European Cup success in 1977. He was also on the mark, this time from open play, in the 1984 final before reverting to his role as spot-kick king as Liverpool won the match on penalties.

A subsequent management career saw Neal in charge at Bolton, Coventry and Manchester City, and he also served as England manager Graham Taylor's right-hand man.

Nicol

Steve Nicol formed part of the backbone of the Liverpool side throughout the 1980s. Initially a defender, he later occupied midfield positions and altogether he made 343 League appearances in the red shirt, scoring on 36 occasions.

Nicol, born in Irvine, Scotland on 11 December 1961, began his career with Ayr United and signed on at Anfield in 1981 for a fee of £300,000. His contribution to the Liverpool side of the 1980s, while not forgotten, is probably not as well remembered as that of the players with whom he starred.

He developed a very useful partnership with John Barnes and, while not building a reputation as a prolific goalscorer himself, he did on one occasion score a hat-trick against Newcastle at St James' Park – and had a fourth goal disallowed in the same game. In 1989, he was voted the PFA's Footballer of the Year.

Having won 27 caps for Scotland, and having played for his country in the 1986 World Cup finals, Nicol left Anfield in 1994. He moved to Notts County as player-coach for a brief period, and then went on to David Pleat's Sheffield Wednesday and to Doncaster Rovers. Later, he took up coaching in the United States, where he still lives and has subsequently moved into commentary.

Owen

Born in Chester on 14 December 1979, Michael Owen supported rivals Everton as a youngster but was spotted playing schools football in Hawarden and signed for Liverpool as an apprentice. His first team debut was a scoring one in May 1997, when he came on as substitute against Wimbledon.

The following season saw Owen become joint top scorer in the Premier League, with international recognition coming against Chile in February 1998 when he became the youngest player to have represented his country in the 20th century. That year's World Cup brought memorable substitute performances in both the initial group matches and against Romania. A spectacular individual goal against Argentina confirmed him as an international force and successor to David Beckham as pin-up and fan favourite.

Having played 297 times for his first club, scoring 158 goals, Owen moved to Real Madrid in 2004 and, having been an automatic choice for club and country, found himself on the bench more often than not.

Owen went on to play for Newcastle, Manchester United and Stoke City but never reached the scoring heights he had shown at Liverpool. On 19 March 2013, Owen announced his retirement from playing at the end of the 2012-13 season.

He finished his international career as England's tenth most-capped player and scored a national record of 26 competitive goals, with 40 in total from 89 appearances, the last in 2008.

But many in the game believe that injuries during the early part of his career meant that he never lived up to expectations after leaving Liverpool.

ABOVE Michael Owen scores for Liverpool in the Worthington Cup Final against Manchester United in 2003

Paisley

Bob Paisley had become part of the Anfield furniture when he was chosen to succeed Bill Shankly as Liverpool manager in 1974. His playing career in red had been unremarkable – he had missed out on the FA Cup Final in 1950 – but as a manager he would become world-famous.

His first season, 1974-75, was a barren one. But when the likes of Phil Neal and Terry McDermott had bedded in alongside local lad Jimmy Case and courageous Emlyn Hughes the League title was there for the taking in 1976.

Next would come the European Cup, the biggest prize of all, and as in 1973 Borussia Moenchengladbach were the opposition, beaten 3-1, this time in Rome. The Reds also retained the Championship at home after a run of 16 games without defeat took them clear of Manchester City, though Kevin Keegan's decision to leave English football for Hamburg was a bitter blow.

Yet even Keegan was replaceable in Paisley's red machine – and Kenny Dalglish, prised from Glasgow giants Celtic for a record £440,000, would make just as big a mark. He slotted into a team in transition, stalwarts like Tommy Smith and John Toshack giving way to the likes of Alan Hansen and David Johnson.

The one disappointment of 1976-77 for Bob Paisley was missing out on the FA Cup – a win against Manchester United, the previous year's runners-

an impossible dream until 1981. Then Liverpool just couldn't stop winning it – four victories in as many years! Another European Cup, the third in five years, was achieved thanks to a rare goal from Alan Kennedy in 1981.

Paisley carried his last trophy back to the boardroom in May 1983 as Liverpool retained the League title. The respect in which he was held was immense, and when he went up Wembley's 39 steps to receive the League Cup that March he was the first manager ever to be awarded such an accolade.

Three European Cups, six League titles, three Milk (League) Cups and a UEFA Cup had made him uniquely successful, a fact the Paisley gates at Anfield celebrate. Bob died in 1996 at the age of 77 but, like Bill Shankly, will never be forgotten.

up, in the final would have brought up a unique treble, but it was not to be. With Dalglish in Keegan's number 7 shirt, a draw was obtained against United in the Charity Shield, but retaining the European Cup was the priority and that was done with a Dalglish goal against Belgian champs Bruges at Wembley.

Another Championship in 1978-79 was achieved with only four games lost and 16 goals conceded – no wonder keeper Ray Clemence was an England squad regular!

The title was retained in 1979-80, though the League Cup would remain

ABOVE Bob Paisley with the League Championship trophy, pictured in 1983

QUOTES

Quotes

Liverpool FC has always been populated by people with opinions. Here are just some of them.

"If you're in the penalty area and don't know what to do with the ball, put it in the net and we'll discuss the options later." **Bob Paisley**

"We've got a lot of Cockneys in the team, but really, it doesn't matter where they're from – we're all playing for Liverpool." **Robbie Fowler**

"I've been on this planet for 45 years, and have supported Liverpool for 42 of them." **Roy Evans**

"Sometimes I feel I'm hardly wanted in this Liverpool team. If I get two or three saves to make, I've had a busy day." **Ray Clemence**

"At Liverpool we never accept second best." **Kenny Dalglish**

"Liverpool are magic, Everton are tragic." **Emlyn Hughes**

"Mind you, I've been here during the bad times too – one year we came second." **Bob Paisley**

"(Bob Paisley) could tell if someone was injured and what the problem was just by watching them walk a few paces. He was never boastful but had great football knowledge. I owe Bob more than I owe anybody else in the game. There will never be another like him." **Kenny Dalglish**

"Shanks was the father figure but Roger Hunt was something special. It might sound daft but just picking up his sweaty kit gave me satisfaction." **Phil Thompson**

"The Liverpool philosophy is simple, and is based on total belief. Maybe that has been the key to Liverpool's consistency. We were taught to go out there, play our own game and fear no one." **Phil Neal**

"Everything seemed to go like clockwork at Liverpool, as though nobody was in charge." **Mark Lawrenson**

"There's no noise like the Anfield noise – and I love it!" **Ian St John**

"We don't have any splits here. The players' country is Liverpool Football Club and their language is football." **Gérard Houllier**

"My life is my work. My work is my life." **Bill Shankly**

"I'd kick my own brother if necessary … it's what being a professional footballer is all about." **Steve McMahon**

"I've just been fortunate enough on my journey to come across top British and European managers like Champions League winner Jose Mourinho and a World Cup winner Luiz Felipe Scolari. But my biggest mentor is myself because I've had to study, so that's been my biggest influence." **Brendan Rogers**

"Nobody likes being criticised, particularly by players who will be in Disneyland this summer on their holidays rather than at the World Cup in Japan." **Phil Thompson responding to criticism from Frank de Boer of Barcelona who said Liverpool were boring**

"I go by records and Bob Paisley is the No 1 manager ever!" **Alan Hansen**

"Liverpool wouldn't be the club it is today without Bill Shankly and Bob Paisley and the players who played there. When I first went there it was a typical Second Division ground and look at it now!" **Ian Callaghan**

On awaiting Everton's arrival for a derby game at Anfield, Bill Shankly gave a box of toilet rolls to the doorman and said: "Give them these when they arrive – they'll need them!"

"The only thing I fear is missing an open goal in front of the Kop. I would die if that were to happen. When they start singing 'You'll Never Walk Alone' my eyes start to water. There have been times when I've actually been crying while I've been playing." **Kevin Keegan**

Records

RIGHT Putting the message over at Anfield

OPPOSITE RIGHT
The liver bird, symbol of a city and of a club

APPEARANCES

Most first team appearances
Ian Callaghan (857)

Most League appearances
Ian Callaghan (640)

Most FA Cup appearances
Ian Callaghan (79)

Most League Cup appearances
Ian Rush (78)

Most European appearances
Jamie Carragher (150)

Oldest player
Ted Doig, 41 years and 165 days v Newcastle United (a) 11 April 1908

Youngest player
Jerome Sinclair, 16 years and six days, v WBA (League Cup), 26 September 2012.

Most seasons as an ever-present
Phil Neal (9)

Most consecutive appearances
Phil Neal (417) 23 October 1976 to 24 September 1983

Longest-serving player
Elisha Scott – 21 years and 52 days, 1913-34

Oldest debutant
Ted Doig, 37 years and 307 days v Burton U (h) 1 September 1904

GOALS

Most first team goals
Ian Rush (346)

Most league goals
Roger Hunt (245)

Most FA Cup goals
Ian Rush (39)

Most League Cup goals
Ian Rush (48)

Most European goals
Steven Gerrard (41)

Highest-scoring substitute
David Fairclough (18)

Most hat-tricks
Gordon Hodgson (17)

Most hat-tricks in a season
Roger Hunt (5 in 1961-62)

Most penalties scored
Steven Gerrard (43)

Most Liverpool games without scoring
Ephraim Longworth (371)

Youngest goalscorer
Ben Woodburn, 17 years and 45 days, v
Leeds United 29 November 2016.

Oldest goalscorer
Billy Liddell, 38 years and 55 days v
Stoke City (h) 5 March 196

INTERNATIONALS

Most capped player
Steven Gerrard (114), England

Most international goals
Michael Owen (26), England
Ian Rush (26), Wales

HONOURS

Most player medals
Phil Neal (20)

WINS AND LOSSES

Record victory
11-0 v Stromgodset, 1974

Record defeat
1-9 v Birmingham City, 1954

TRANSFER FEES
(as of 1 July 2019)

Record transfer fee paid
£75m for Virgil van Dijl 2018

Record transfer fee received
£142m for Philippe Coutinho,
2018

Reina

The hair-raising feats of bald-headed stopper Pepe Reina have made him a legend at Liverpool with nearly 400 games in goal.

Signed by Benitez in 2005, his first season ended with an FA Cup final against West Ham, and his habit of saving spot kicks made him an instant hero. Three out of four of West Ham's penalties were blocked and the Cup was heading to Anfield for the seventh time.

Reina was to soon create a new club record. His shut-out against Blackburn in April 2007 was his 28th in his first 50 league games - three more than the Kop's king keeper Ray Clemence.

The maturing goalie continued to go from strength to strength over the coming seasons at Anfield and delighted fans by penning a new six-year contract in April 2010. "It's probably the best news of my life that I'll be here for the next six years. To play for Liverpool is very special. My kids enjoy it and they have picked up the Scouse accent already. I am really proud of that. In the years ahead they will speak much more Scouse too."

A month later, Kopites voted Reina the Player of the Season for 2009-10 ahead of what would be a triumphant summer when his country seized their first World Cup trophy although he didn't play in the Final but was a vital squad player.

The seasons that followed would prove frustrating as Liverpool continued to miss out on Champions League football, but Reina stayed loyal and in February 2012 was rewarded with a medal following a Carling Cup final win over Cardiff City at Wembley.

Pepe played for Napoli on loan during 2013-14 and re-joined them a year later after a season as back up at Bayern Munich. Following a further century plus of Serie A appearances he moved to AC Milan in 2018.

First capped by Spain in 2005 Reina has been a member of his country's squad at many major tournaments, including the 2008 and 2012 Euros and the 2010 FIFA World Cup, all of which saw him collect winner's medals.

Robertson

Signed for a bargain £8m from Hull City in the summer of 2017, Andy was initially brought in to compete with Alberto Moreno but it didn't take the Glaswegian long to firmly establish himself as first choice. Defensively solid, his attacking ability makes him a powerful weapon. Robertson's ability to provide sumptuous crosses while on the run contributed to him being credited with 11 Premier League assists in the 2018-19 season, a tally bettered by only four players, including Trent Alexander-Arnold who managed 12. Both full backs were two of four Liverpool men included in the PFA Team of the Year.

Having come through the Celtic youth system, Robertson began life in senior football with Queen's Park in 2012-13 and was quickly snapped up by Dundee United after his first season. Such was his success at Tannadice that like Queen's Park, Dundee United couldn't hold on to Robertson for longer than one season in the first team. Former Burnley manager Stan Ternent was chief scout for Hull City and persuaded the Tigers to pay a reported £2.85m to bring south a player who had just become a full international.

While Hull struggled, Robertson thrived in the Premier League – and scored for Scotland against England shortly after coming into English football - but his time at the KC Stadium was punctuated by constant changed of level. Relegated in his first season, Hull bounced back immediately via the Play offs only to be instantly relegated again. While his club struggled Robertson had shown he was Premier League quality and remained in the top flight after Liverpool stepped in.

LEFT Andy Robertson at the victory parade for Liverpool after winning the UEFA Champions League Final in 2019.

Rush

Striker supreme Ian Rush was born on
20 October 1961 at St Asaph, near Rhyl
in North Wales. He began his career
with local side Chester City, which he
would later manage after he hung up
his boots, but was soon spotted by Bob
Paisley and was on his way to Liverpool
for £300,000 – then a record fee for a
teenager.

He made his debut in red against
Ipswich in December 1980 and, between
then and 1987, during Liverpool
Football Club's golden era, he was to
score a quite remarkable 139 goals in
224 League matches. One can only
imagine the feelings of dedicated Reds
fans when Rush decided to leave Anfield
in favour of Juventus, following in the
footsteps of countryman John Charles.
It proved, however, to be a good move
for Liverpool, as they netted £2.75m

apiece in 1986 and 1989 and one in 1992, all for the winning side) is an all-time best.

Rush also continued to score freely for Wales. In all, he made 73 appearances for his country, scoring a record 28 goals and ensuring himself legendary status. He moved to Leeds United in 1996, and to Newcastle a year later, but the goalscoring days were by now largely over. Wrexham (where he was player-coach) and Sydney Olympic in Australia were further stops before retirement.

Rush scored an impressive 346 goals in 658 senior outings for Liverpool, although his total of League goals fell a scant 16 short of Roger Hunt's club record 245.

and, in any case, Rush came back within the year. He just couldn't settle abroad and pined for the scene of his former glories.

His second spell at the club, which lasted until 1996, saw him score slightly less prolifically, but he still managed a further 90 strikes in 245 League encounters. During his career, Rush also scored 44 goals in the FA Cup, 39 for Liverpool, which constitutes a 20th century record. His five-goal haul in FA Cup Finals (two

Rush's 49 League Cup goals equals Geoff Hurst. He scored 10 times in 18 Wembley outings with Liverpool, won the League Cup five times, collected five Championship medals and one European Cup and was awarded the MBE.

He's back at Anfield now, as the club's soccer schools ambassador and also putting in some work with the commercial department.

Salah

Scoring 44 times in his first season with Liverpool, being the fastest Liverpool player to score 50 goals for the club and scoring more goals (69) than any other Reds player ever has in his first 100 games for Liverpool are just some of the records Mo Salah established.

It wasn't simply the sheer volume of goals that the Egyptian magician conjured but the magical style in which so many of them were scored. Elegantly balanced, swift of feet and able to score with either foot (No one has scored as many left-footed goals as the 25 he tucked away in 2017-18 – out of a total of 44), Salah has been a sensational signing by Liverpool, now worth much more than the then club record paid in June 2017- a fee that eventually reached £50m.

Salah has previously played in the Premier League for Chelsea who he had scored against home and away in Champions League wins for Basel shortly before signing for the London club. However, Mo started just six Premier League games and 10 in total for the Blues for whom he also came off the bench a total of nine times, being discarded by Jose Mourinho after he featured in an infamous 2-4 home FA Cup defeat by Bradford City in 2015.

Loaned to Fiorentina Salah soon found form, a brace in a 2-1 away win over Juventus giving him six goals in as many games shortly after joining the Viola, one of which came in a Europa Cup win over Spurs. It wouldn't be his last European goal against Tottenham – and it wasn't the first either as he had scored against them for Basel.

Although Fiorentina wanted to keep Salah under the terms of an 18-month loan agreement with Chelsea, instead the player signed up with Roma, again initially on loan. His first return to Florence brought victory, a goal and a red card and there was evidently a point to prove when Fiorentina came to the Eternal City for the return, as Mo netted twice (and picked up a yellow card) in a 4-1 victory.

While with Roma Salah scored twice in the Rome derby as Lazio were beaten 3-2, and claimed a Serie A hat-trick against Bologna as well as gaining the experience of big Champions League clashes with Barcelona and Real Madrid.

Perhaps that earlier spell at Chelsea helped Mo as he knew what to expect when coming into the Premier League with Liverpool. Whereas so many overseas stars need time to acclimatize Salah was an instant hit. A debut goal at Watford became the first of six games in which Salah would score in his first nine outings. The goals kept coming at an incredible rate with the return fixture with Watford seeing Salah score four in a 5-0 thrashing.

Another hat-trick came in his second season at Bournemouth, a season where he was the joint top scorer in the Premier League (With Sadio Mane and Arsenal's Pierre-Emerick Aubameyang on 22 goals). The climax of that season came when Mo despatched an early penalty in the Champions League final against Spurs, a year after he had limped out of the same show-piece occasion after half an hour. That was a sad end to a season in which he had achieved the double of being Player of the Year for both the PFA and Football Writers' Association.

A host of other awards included not only being Liverpool's Player of the Year but also the African Player of the Year. Born in Nagrig, Basyoun in Egypt on 15 June 1992, Mo began with El Mokawloon in Cairo before moving to Switzerland with Basel at whose ground he had scored twice as a sub for Egypt Under 23s in a game against Basel a month before his 20th birthday.

Having joined Basel Salah started with a debut in the Champions League. Going on to play in the Europa League in his first season he went on to score against both Spurs and Chelsea, scoring against the Blues again the following season while also winning the Swiss Super League in successive seasons in 2013 and 2014.

Internationally Salah is Egypt's best ever footballer. As a 20-year old with Basel he played in the UK at the 2012 Olympics. He scored in all three group games at the Millennium Stadium, Old Trafford and Hampden Park before playing in the losing quarter-final with Japan, again at Old Trafford.

A full international from September 2011 he was runner up at the African Cup of Nations in 2017 when he was named in the Team of the Tournament. A year later despite not being fully fit following the Champions League final Salah managed to play and score at the World Cup finals in Russia.

figures. Indeed, to many, Scott is revered as the club's best-ever keeper.

Agile and courageous, Scott played a major role – and missed a mere three League games – as Liverpool claimed the League title in 1921-22 and was ever present between the sticks the following season as the Championship was retained.

He gained the first of 31 caps for Northern Ireland in 1920, the last of which was earned at the age of 40, two years after leaving Liverpool.

Scott's duels with Everton's legendary centre-forward Dixie Dean were a key feature of the derby matches of their era, with the Reds' keeper constantly reminding the Blues what they had missed out on – he was recommended to Everton before going to Anfield but turned down for being too young. Everton came in for him towards the end of his career but Liverpool fans wrote sacks of protest letters and Scott stayed put until he asked for a move back home to become player-manager of Belfast Celtic.

Elisha Scott died in May 1959.

ABOVE Elisha Scott saves a penalty, against Arsenal, 1923

Scott

Had it not been for World War I, goalkeeper Elisha Scott (born 24 August 1894) would have played well over 500 games for the club. As it was, his Liverpool career spanned a remarkable 21 years from his debut on New Year's Day, 1913 – a 0-0 draw at Newcastle – to his final appearance, a 2-0 away defeat to Chelsea, in February 1934. By then he'd clocked up 467 first-team appearances and he remains one of the club's iconic

Shankly

The arrival of Scot Bill Shankly from Huddersfield as manager in December 1959 came after nearly a decade outside the top flight. Rivals Everton prospered until 'Shanks' woke the sleeping giant.

He built slowly but methodically, fashioning his side round a central backbone of his countrymen. Goalkeeper Tommy Lawrence, centre-back Ron Yeats and striker Ian St John all hailed from north of the border, and all possessed the qualities of skill, strength and determination Shankly expected of his men.

They'd bring top-flight football back to Anfield in 1962, going on to win the League two years later and – finally – the FA Cup in 1965. Their beaten opponents Leeds, managed by the dour Don Revie, would prove to be constant rivals for the coming decade.

Shankly had long been used to making headlines, but when he announced Liverpool's record buy, £200,000 Ray Kennedy from Arsenal in July 1974, just months after a second FA Cup win, he used the event to announce he was quitting while he was on top.

To the city of Liverpool he was a legend, even if the blue half's respect was grudging, and his death at the age of 68 in 1981 – less than a year after another mighty Merseysider, John Lennon – was universally mourned.

LEFT Shanks salutes the crowd at Wembley after Liverpool had defeated Leeds in the FA Cup Final, 1965

BELOW Bill Shankly pictured in 1969

SHANKS' WIT AND WISDOM

"Some people believe football is a matter of life and death. I am very disappointed with that attitude. I can assure you it is much, much more important than that."

"Napoleon wanted to conquer the bloody world. I wanted Liverpool to be untouchable."

"No one was asked to do more than anyone else … we were a team. We shared the ball, we shared the game, we shared the worries."

"I was the best manager in Britain because I was never devious or cheated anyone. I'd break my wife's legs if I played against her, but I'd never cheat her."

"I think Dixie would be amazed to know that even in death he could draw a bigger crowd than Everton can on a Saturday afternoon."
At Dixie Dean's funeral

"The 'This is Anfield' plaque is there to remind our lads who they're playing for, and to remind the opposition who they're playing against."

"The problem with you, son, is that all your brains are in your head."
To a Liverpool trainee

"If Everton were playing at the bottom of the garden, I'd pull the curtains."

"The fans here are the greatest in the land. They know the game and they know what they want to see. The people on the Kop make you feel great – yet humble."

"Of course I didn't take my wife to see Rochdale as an anniversary present, it was her birthday. Would I have got married in the football season? Anyway, it was Rochdale reserves."

Smith

It's hard to imagine that Tommy Smith – uncompromising in the tackle and the toughest defender in the business – joined Liverpool from school as an inside forward. Then again, years later, in what was supposed to be his final game for the club – the 1977 European Cup Final – he demonstrated all the hallmarks of a canny striker with a magnificent header that turned the game Liverpool's way.

The 'Anfield Iron', born on 5 April 1945, signed for the Reds on his 17th birthday and made his first team bow against Birmingham the following May. During his early days, Bill Shankly used to send Smith into action in the number 10 shirt – remember, these were the days when numbers reflected the players' positions. The ploy especially bamboozled foreign opponents, who expected him to play much further upfield than he did.

An FA Cup success, Liverpool's first, came in 1965 as Smith became a fixture in the side, not only surviving a Shanks rebuilding phase but becoming club captain. Shankly recognized Smith's leadership qualities – suggesting that the rugged defender wasn't born, but quarried!

As his eventual total of 637 Liverpool appearances stacked up, so did the winners' medals. He won four First Division titles, two FA Cups, two European Cups (although he missed the 1978 Final after dropping a pickaxe on his foot!), two UEFA Cups and a European Super Cup.

Smith won one England cap, against Wales in 1971, and was awarded an MBE in 1977. He played out his career at Swansea City. In later life Tommy suffered with Alzheimer's disease. He passed away in April 2019, aged 74.

ABOVE Tommy Smith pictured in action for Liverpool, 1970

Graham Souness, captain of Liverpool, and Di Bartolomei, captain of AS Roma exchange club pennants before the start of the European Cup Final, 1984

Souness

The career of Graham Souness has been marked by controversy. Born in Edinburgh on 6 May 1953, the midfielder initially joined Spurs, but was signed by Bob Paisley from Middlesbrough for £350,000 in 1978.

He had been a hero at Ayresome Park, and for a long time he was a hero at Anfield. Totally committed to the cause, he helped Liverpool win the European Cup three times, the League Championship five times and the League Cup four times. Between 1978 and 1984 he scored 38 goals in 247 League appearances.

As his playing career then drew to a close, he moved to Rangers as player-manager. Apart from being sent off in his first game, he did well there, but Anfield called him back and he returned as manager in 1991. His attempts to revamp an ageing squad were, however, largely doomed to failure, and an FA Cup defeat by Bristol City in 1994 proved to be the final straw.

Since then, Souness has had a quite remarkable managerial career, if only for the number of clubs with which he has been involved. After Anfield, he moved to the cauldron of Turkey's Galatasaray. Then he returned to England to manage Southampton, before helping Torino return to Italy's top division.

After that it was Benfica, Blackburn and Newcastle who he left in 2006. Nowadays Souness is as feisty a pundit as he was a player.

Birkenhead, it features a grand terrace punctuated by imposing shelters with expansive bedding schemes once highlighted by fountains.

The 45-hectare park opened in 1870 and contains the Gladstone Conservatory (Grade II), built in 1899 by Mackenzie and Moncur, who had also constructed the Palm House in Sefton Park.

The whole landscape of Stanley Park will change radically with the construction of the Reds' proposed new stadium, but the phrase 'across the Park' will never be lost from Liverpool folklore.

LEFT AND BELOW
Stanley Park, on a beautiful summer's day

Stanley Park

Stanley Park, the swathe of green that separates Anfield and Goodison, is one of Liverpool's largest and grandest open spaces. It's one of a trio of great Victorian parks – Newsham (1868), Stanley (1870) and Sefton (1872) – that opened within five years and is arguably the most architecturally significant.

Landscaped by Edward Kemp, who had assisted Paxton at Chatsworth and

ABOVE Steve Staunton tackles Kevin Gallacher of Blackburn Rovers

RIGHT Staunton at full stretch for Liverpool. He was appointed Republic of Ireland manager in 2006

Staunton

Kenny Dalglish signed Steve Staunton (born January 1969) from Irish side Dundalk in 1986. The full-back made his Reds debut in a 1-1 draw with Spurs in 1988 and soon after gained the first of 102 international caps for the Republic of Ireland.

Impressive performances at left-back meant that the young Staunton held his place in a very good Liverpool side, one that reached the 1989 FA Cup Final and gained a 3-2 extra-time victory over Everton. Arsenal dramatically put paid to hopes of a double, but the League title was theirs the following season.

On the international scene, Staunton was ever present for the Republic of Ireland as they reached the quarter-finals of the 1990 World Cup. But he was sold to Aston Villa by Graeme Souness in 1991 for more than £1m.

He enjoyed more success with Villa, winning the a League Cup winners' medal in 1994, and gained further international recognition at USA '94.

As his contract with Villa petered out, Staunton decided to return to Anfield and in a two-year spell he took his appearances total for the Reds to 147 – weighing in with six goals – before moving back to Villa Park. He later turned to management, although his stints as boss of the Irish national side and of Darlington could not be termed great successes.

St John

Motherwell-born Ian St John began with his hometown club in 1956 at the age of 18. The 'Well were happy enough to sell him to Liverpool in 1961, but Bill Shankly had trouble persuading the board that, at £37,500, St John was a good investment.

He did sign him however, and the striker proved to be a very good investment indeed. An excellent reader of the game, St John had both style and pace. As well as providing dozens of goals for his striking partners, he went on to score 118 times in 426 appearances overall. Although standing only five feet seven and a half inches, he had great aerial ability due to his marvellous sense of timing.

During his career, he played 21 times for Scotland. It would have been more had Scottish management at that time been less reluctant to include England-based players in the international side.

Playing alongside Roger Hunt and later in midfield, St John became yet another Liverpool legend. While at Anfield, he had his own radio show and it was clear that he was a natural broadcaster. When he finished play-ing, he tried his hand at management with Motherwell and Portsmouth, but then began a new career in television. He became particularly famous for the Saint and Greavsie show on ITV.

BELOW Ian St John pictured in 1968

Stubbins

The only footballer on the cover of Sergeant Pepper's Lonely Hearts Club Band, Albert Stubbins was Liverpool's record signing in 1946 when he cost £13,000 from Newcastle who he played for before the Second World War.

A centre-forward of devastating pace who liked to leather home a shot with his size 11 boots, Stubbins a made scoring debut in September 1946. This set him on the way to becoming an important member of the Liverpool team who took the title that season, Stubbins being joint top scorer on 24 goals with Jack Balmer. Albert equalled his tally again a year later and went on to play for Liverpool in the FA Cup final in 1950.

He also played in that year's semi-final against Everton, a team he could have easily joined instead of Liverpool. Both Merseyside clubs had agreed a fee of £13,000 with Newcastle United. Stubbins was at the Newcastle News Theatre when United asked for a message to be put on screen saying, 'Would Albert Stubbins please report to St. James' Park.' Stubbins was to explain that when he got there he was told representatives of both clubs were there to meet him and he was asked who he'd like to speak to

first. Stubbins tossed a coin to decide and saw the Reds first. Suitably impressed Albert signed for Liverpool without even hearing what Everton had to say.

A native of Wallsend Stubbins scored a total of 83 goals in 178 games for Liverpool before finishing his career with Ashington in 1953-54. Before joining Newcastle he had been a young player before the war with Whitley & Monkseaton as well as Sunderland and played as a 'Guest' for the Wearsiders a couple of times during the war when he also claimed no fewer than 29 hat-tricks as part of his tally of over 230 war-time goals for the Magpies.

In representative football Albert had one unofficial appearance for England and was on Liverpool's books when he scored five times for the Football League against the Irish League in 1950.

From 1954-60 Stubbins scouted for Liverpool before going to the USA to coach New York Americans and Trenton Grade School. While a Tynesider by birth on 13 July 1919, in 1923 his family had moved to America and he was raised in New York and later Detroit before returning to England.

In later life he became a journalist for The People, became a broadcaster and lived on the north-east coast until his death between Christmas and New Year in 2002.

ABOVE Stubbins scored a total of 83 goals in 178 games for Liverpool

ABOVE Suárez takes on Distin of Everton

Suárez

In the end it was Liverpool who had bitten off more than they could chew when they parted company with Luis Suarez after the player joined Barcelona following his disgraceful exit from the World Cup in the summer of 2014.

He will remembered as one of the club's greatest ever players but it became impossible to keep him once he expressed his desire to leave for Spain and had been banned for a third biting offence during the tournament in Brazil.

He had joined Liverpool from Ajax on deadline day in January 2011 and wasn't phased one bit by wearing Liverpool's famous No.7 shirt. Like Keegan and Dalglish before him, he became an Anfield idol and scored some of the most spectacular goals ever seen by the fans.

Born in Uruguay where he quickly established a reputation as a deadly goalscorer, Suárez moved to the Netherlands to play for Gronningen before transferring to Ajax in 2007.

He was made the club captain the following year and became the league's top scorer with 35 goals in 33 games and was named Dutch Footballer of the Year.

In the 2010-2011 season, he scored his hundredth Ajax goal, joining an elite group of players including Johan Cruyff, Macro van Basten and Dennis Bergkamp.

Suarez scored 17 goals in 39 appearances during his first full season in Merseyside, including the equaliser as Liverpool defeated neighbours Everton in the FA Cup semi-final. Another highlight was a superlative hat-trick at Carrow Road which included a 45-yard lob. He also ended the campaign with a League Cup medal.

The Uruguayan found the target 30 times in all competitions during a remarkable 2012-13 season and received the Standard Chartered Player of the Season award by a landslide majority.

Having registered a ratio of more than a goal a game with a series of phenomenal displays in the first half of the next campaign, Suarez signed a new long-term contract with the club in December 2013.

On 22 March 2014, he scored his sixth Premier League hat-trick for the club, making him the most frequent scorer of hat-tricks in Premier League history. On 27 April 2014 he won the PFA Players' Player of the Year award, becoming the first non-European to win the award.

Suárez is also Uruguay's all-time record goal-scorer with 40 goals in less than 80 games although, inevitably, his international career has been tainted with controversy.

In the 2010 World Cup, he infamously blocked an extra time goal bound header with his hands during the quarter-finals against Ghana who subsequently missed the penalty and lost the tie.

He has also been involved in three biting incidents in his career, the latest in a group World Cup match against Italy in Brazil in June 2014 for which he received a lengthy ban.

With more than 80 goals in just 133 appearances for Liverpool, he will be a very hard act to follow and his departure was only made slightly easier to swallow by an enormous £75 million fee which was used to invest on quality players of the likes of Adam Lallana, Emre Can and Lazar Markovic.

Thompson

Seventeen-year-old Liverpudlian Phil Thompson signed professional forms in 1971 for the club he had supported as a boy. Another of the players to win a host of medals during Liverpool's golden period, the tall young central defender was soon to repay Bill Shankly, and then Bob Paisley, for the faith they showed in him.

Thompson was an Anfield player until 1984, during which time he made 340 League appearances and scored seven goals. He also appeared for his country on 42 occasions,

playing a pivotal role in the England defence. Strong and intelligent, he soon became a favourite of the Kop – where he had stood as a boy. He gained the nickname 'Pinocchio' due to his larger than average proboscis.

After seeing out his playing days at Sheffield United, his career having been cut short by recurring injuries, Thompson returned to Anfield in a coaching capacity. He fell out with the management, but later returned as assistant to Gérard Houllier, taking over from the Frenchman for half a season when he became ill. He spent several months leaping about in the dugout and, at away grounds, cries of 'We love Pinocchio' (Italian operatic arias have a lot to answer for) turned to 'Sit down, Pinocchio'.

Thompson now spends Saturdays in the ranks of the Sky TV pundits.

ABOVE Goalmouth action as Liverpool play Chelsea at Stamford Bridge on their way to another title in 1947

RIGHT Ronnie Rosenthal, Ian Rush, Ronnie Whelan, Alan Hansen and John Barnes celebrate winning the League in 1990

Titles

Liverpool won their first League title in 1900-01, a last-game win against bottom club West Bromwich putting them ahead of all-conquering Sunderland, following a season when they themselves had been pipped by Aston Villa.

Further League titles came in 1906, 1922, 1923 and 1947, with just a single season in the then Division Two in 1904-05 spoiling their ever-present record in the English football elite.

Stars of this period included fearless goalkeeper Elisha Scott, skilful striker Albert Stubbins and flying winger Billy Liddell, who served from 1945 to 1961.

The 1963-64 season saw the Reds' first title under Bill Shankly, and they repeated the feat in 1965-66 and 1972-73, before Bob Paisley's remarkable run of success.

This saw Liverpool bring home the top prize in 1976, 1977, 1979, 1980, 1982 and 1983. Joe Fagan's side achieved the title in 1984, with the final three Championships to date, in 1986 (the League and Cup Double), 1988 and 1990, being won under Kenny Dalglish's player-managership. The total number of title wins is an impressive 18.

The Top 10

LEAGUE APPEARANCES

Rank	Player	Years	Apps
1	Ian Callaghan	(1959-1978)	640
2	Jamie Carragher	(1996–2014)	508
3	Steven Gerrard	(1998-2015)	504
4	Billy Liddell	(1945-1961)	492
5	Emlyn Hughes	(1966-1979)	474
6	Ray Clemence	(1968-1981)	470
7	Ian Rush	(1980-1996)	469
8	Tommy Smith	(1962-1978)	467
9	Phil Neal	(1974-1986)	455
10	Bruce Grobbelaar	(1981-1994)	440

ALL COMPETITIONS

Rank	Player	Years	Apps
1	Ian Callaghan	(1960-1978)	857
2	Jamie Carragher	(1996–2014)	737
3	Steven Gerrard	(1998-2015)	710
4=	Ray Clemence	(1968-1981)	665
4=	Emlyn Hughes	(1966-1979)	665
6	Ian Rush	(1980-1996)	660
7	Phil Neal	(1974-1986)	650
8	Tommy Smith	(1962-1978	638
9	Bruce Grobbelaar	(1981-1994)	628
10	Alan Hansen	(1977-1990)	620

LEAGUE SCORERS

Rank	Player	Years	Goals
1	Roger Hunt	(1959-1970)	244
2	Gordon Hodgson	(1925-1936)	233
3	Ian Rush	(1980-1996)	229
4	Billy Liddell	(1945-1961)	215
5	Harry Chambers	(1919-1928)	135
6	Robbie Fowler	(1993-2006)	128
7	Jack Parkinson	(1899-1914)	123
8=	Steven Gerrard	(1998-2015)	120
8=	Sam Raybould	(1899-1907)	120
10=	Kenny Dalglish	(1977-1990)	118
10=	Michael Owen	(1919-1927)	118

OVERALL SCORERS

Rank	Player	Years	Goals
1	Ian Rush	(1980-1996)	346
2	Roger Hunt	(1959-1970)	285
3	Gordon Hodgson	(1925-1936)	241
4	Billy Liddell	(1945-1961)	228
5	Steven Gerrard	(1998–2015)	186
6	Robbie Fowler	(1993-2001)	183
7	Kenny Dalglish	(1977-1990)	172
8	Michael Owen	(1997-2004)	158
9	Harry Chambers	(1919-1928)	151
10	Sam Raybould	(1900–1907)	130

Torres

Fernando Torres burst upon the Premiership like no other foreign player had ever done. He scored 24 Premiership goals in 33 appearances for his new employers which, coupled with nine goals in the Carling Cup and Champions League, ensured he became the most prolific player from outside these shores in his debut season, overtaking Ruud van Nistelrooy's record.

Torres, born on 20 March 1984 in Madrid, was a promising youngster whose talents were spotted early on and he joined Atletico Madrid in 1995 at the age of 11, signing a first contract with his boyhood heroes four years later. Despite suffering a broken leg earlier in

the season, he made his debut in May 2001 and went on to make 214 League appearances for the Spanish side, scoring 82 times, before his July 2007 transfer to Liverpool for a fee of around £20 million. The deal smashed the club's previous record of £14 million paid to Auxerre for Djibril Cissé.

Idolised by the Kop for his scoring record, with 81 goals in 142 appearances in all competitions, it was a shock when he moved to Chelsea in January 2011 although the £50 million fee softened the blow.

Indeed it proved to be a shrewd piece of business as Torres failed to find his Liverpool form at Chelsea and scored just 45 goals in 172 appearances by the end of the 2013/14 season.

Although he did win an FA Cup, Europa Cup and Champions League medal at Chelsea, he finally returned to Spain (where he has also won 110 caps) to play for his first club Atletico Madrid.

LEFT Fernando Torres is welcomed to Liverpool by Rafael Benitez

BELOW Torres evades a Reading tackle

RIGHT John Toshack
playing for Liverpool
in 1972

BELOW John
Toshack and Kevin
Keegan, attacking the
Tottenham Hotspur
goal, 1977

Toshack

John Benjamin Toshack was born in Cardiff on 22 March 1949. He began his career as a forward with Cardiff City (75 goals in 162 League appearances) before moving to Anfield in November 1970. At the time, he was Liverpool's most expensive signing, costing the club £110,000.

It was a while before he established himself at his new home, but when he did, he was formed a marvellous double act with Kevin Keegan.

Toshack, who was enormously strong and had great aerial power, scored on 74 occasions during 172 League appearances for Liverpool, before moving to Swansea City as player-manager in 1978. Perhaps influenced by Swansea's long-dead bard, Dylan Thomas, he started to write poetry himself.

Rather more importantly however, as manager, he guided his new club from the Fourth to the First Division. Swansea were more or less bankrupted in the process and could not afford to pay top-flight wages to the players. Toshack moved on.

Having played for Wales on 40 occasions, he was later to manage the Welsh side. But first, his managerial skills took Real Sociedad to their first Spanish Cup win and Real Madrid to a Spanish League championship. He went on to manage a host of Spanish clubs.

Toshak had spells as manager of the Welsh national team and has been a become a bit of a managerial nomad. He was last seen in Morocco and East Azerbaijan.

Trebles

In 1984 Joe Fagan, an Anfield boot room regular since 1958, was bidding to emulate Huddersfield and Arsenal, the only teams ever to win three successive Championships. In the event he not only succeeded but went one better than previous manager Bob Paisley by adding the Milk and European Cups in a unique Treble.

The power on the pitch was provided by combative Scots midfielder Graeme Souness, a 350-game veteran who never, ever admitted a cause was lost. The icing on the cake was that Everton had been the Milk Cup Finalists in the first of three all-Merseyside Wembley Finals in that decade.

Liverpool's other Treble came in Gérard Houllier's time at Anfield as manager. The Worthington Cup was won in February 2001 – the club's first trophy in six years – to be followed in rapid succession by the FA Cup (against Arsenal), UEFA Cup (against Alaves), Community Shield (against Manchester United) and European Super Cup (Bayern Munich).

Such a stunning success rate was impossible to maintain, of course, but having endured the famine Anfield's faithful were happy to gorge themselves at the feast.

ABOVE Robbie Fowler, Steven Gerrard, manager Gérard Houllier and Sami Hyypia display Liverpool's three trophies, the UEFA Cup, Worthington Cup and FA Cup, on a parade through the streets of Liverpool, 2001

UEFA Cup

Having reached the European Cup Winners' Cup Final in Glasgow in 1965, only to lose narrowly to Borussia Dortmund of Germany, the Reds and their fans were hungry for more. Yet success in European competition under Bill Shankly eluded them for some time.

The first silverware was obtained in 1973 when a two-legged UEFA Cup Final saw them facing German opposition once more in Borussia Moenchengladbach. Inspirational Kevin Keegan scored twice to help his team to a 3-0 home lead, and though Moenchengladbach prevailed in

Germany, Liverpool hung on to take the trophy with a 3-2 aggregate.

They won the Cup for the second time against Bruges in 1976, again after a hard-fought two-legged tie, squeezing home on a 4-3 aggregate. Bob Paisley was now in command.

Liverpool have won more European trophies than any other English team with six European Cups, three UEFA Cups, and three UEFA Super Cups. As the 2019-20 season began Liverpool were within nine games of having played 400 competitive fixtures in European competition. Over 200 of these have been in the Champions League or its predecessor the European Cup. Over 100 have been in the Europa League or its predecessor the UEFA Cup and there were 29 in the former European Cup Winners' Cup as well as 22 in the old Inter-Cities Fairs Cup as well as seven Super Cup meetings.

Van Dijk

ABOVE Van Dijk lining up for The Netherlands

A cool £75m was a world record for a defender when Liverpool were reported to have paid that sum to Southampton for Virgil Van Dijk in January 2018 but it quickly became apparent that this was an astute investment in a player who in 2019 was named UEFA Men's Player of the Year and runner up to Lionel Messi as the FIFA Men's Player of the Year.

Van Dijk's first full season at Anfield in 2018-19 saw him collect a cabinet full of individual awards to go with the Champions League medal he won during the season. Voted the PFA Players' Player of the Year, Virgil took the equivalent award at Liverpool as well as being the Premier League Player of the Season, a member of the PFA team of the Year and making the UEFA Nations League Team of the Tournament.

A goal against Everton on his Liverpool debut five days after joining the club on New Year's Day 2018 made Van Dijk the first player since 1901 (Bill White) to debut in the Merseyside derby and score.

Having helped his new club to the Champions League final against Real Madrid in his first few months he went one better in 2019 helping Liverpool to a clean sheet in the final as Tottenham were tamed.

were 55 appearances for Groningen, ending in May 2013 with a Play-off defeat to FC Twente as Groningen competed for a European place.

The following month a fee reported to be £2.6m took Van Dijk to Celtic where he won back to back SPL titles in 2013-14 when he was the club's Player of the Year - and 2014-15, with the Scottish League Cup also coming his way in his second season.

It had been Martin Koeman who had scouted Van Dijk for Groningen and his son Ronald who subsequently signed him for Southampton in 2015, this time for £13m. He continued to excel at St. Mary's, being named Player of the Year in his first season and becoming captain in his second.

Made captain of the Netherlands three months after joining Liverpool, Van Dijk hails from Breda, where he was born on 8 July 1991. As a young player he spent time with Willem II before joining Groningen for whom he debuted on 1 May 2011. There

Venison

Like his left-back predecessor, Alan Kennedy, Barry Venison played much of his football in his native north-east, for Sunderland and Newcastle. In between times, the blond bombshell managed to play more than 150 games for Liverpool, in the process gaining two League Championships and an FA Cup winners' medal as part of the all-conquering team of Kenny Dalglish.

Having written to Liverpool (and all the other top-flight clubs) letting them know of his impending availability, he signed at the end of his Sunderland contract in summer 1986 for £250,000.

Venison had already captained his former club to the Milk (League) Cup Final in 1985, the youngest player ever to skipper a side in a Wembley showpiece at 20 years and 220 days.

His six years at Anfield were greatly hampered by injury, and the arrival of

Graeme Souness saw Venison on the move again. Having joined Newcastle in 1992 for another £250,000 fee, he was moved by manager Kevin Keegan from full-back to midfield and as a result won a pair of England caps – at the age of 30 – to add to his Liverpool honours.

After brief spells in Turkey with Galatasaray and, later, Southampton, Barry hung up his boots to become a TV pundit. He now lives in California.

ABOVE Barry Venison shields the ball from Mark Robins of Manchester United during the FA Charity Shield, 1990

Watson

Tom Watson was the first man to bring the league title to Liverpool. He had previous. He had been the man behind Sunderland's 'Team of All The Talents' who won the league three times in four years during the 1890s, when his Scots dominated side were runners' up in the fourth of those seasons.

Watson was tempted to Anfield in the summer of 1896 by the offer of a salary of £300 per year, joining Liverpool on 17 August after accepting the club's offer on 25 July. He remained with the club for 19 years, setting a record which remains intact as Liverpool's longest serving manager. When Watson arrived Liverpool's only season in the top flight had resulted in relegation but Watson was to transform them into winners. Tom's team took the title in 1901 and 1906 having gone within a whisker of taking it in 1899.

Born in Byker in Newcastle on 8 April 1859 Watson managed Newcastle United precursors Newcastle West End and also Newcastle East End before coming to Sunderland. He passed away on May 15th 1915 aged only 56, dying as a result of pneumonia and pleurisy. He is buried in Anfield cemetery, a few yards away from goalkeeper Ned Doig who he brought with him from Sunderland. Watson's grave was unmarked until the centenary of his death when the club historians of Liverpool and Sunderland got together to erect a headstone. The ceremony was attended by Sunderland's ambassador Jim Montgomery and Liverpool's Sunderland born Alan Kennedy.

Whelan

Ronnie Whelan, originally a rabid Manchester United fan, was born in Dublin on 25 September 1961. Spotted by a Liverpool scout in Ireland, he was signed by the ever-astute Bob Paisley for a very small fee, and he moved to Anfield in 1979. From 1983 onwards, he was a vital member of the side that won almost everything.

Never a prolific goalscorer, Whelan's talent was that of a ball-winner and link man. He operated mainly from the left side of midfield, and often featured in the rapid counter-attacking moves for which Liverpool were famous at the time.

He scored 73 goals in almost 500 matches, but his tackling ability also sometimes saw him occupying a defensive role. Whelan had tremendous stamina and enthusiasm, was willing to learn and proved extremely adaptable. In other words, he was a true professional.

ABOVE Ronnie Whelan lifts the FA Cup in 1989 after defeating Everton

Whelan played 53 times for the Republic of Ireland between 1981 and 1995, making his debut in April 1981 in a game against Czechoslovakia.

Stricken by injury towards the end of his playing career, he moved to Southend United in 1994, later becoming player-manager. He then tried club management in Greece and subsequently became known as an erudite after-dinner speaker as well as a personable TV pundit.

World Club Championship

The World Club Cup, also known as the Intercontinental Cup and the Toyota Cup, is a match played in Japan between the club champions of Europe and South America. It was inaugurated in 1960 by a match between Spanish side Real Madrid and Uruguayan club Peñarol and was created (as the Intercontinental Cup) by Henri Delauney as a way of determining the top club in the world, Europe and South America being the top football continents.

It is not generally considered by European clubs to be a particularly prestigious event, but this may be because South American teams have nearly always won. At all events, as European Champions in 1977, Liverpool elected not to take part. They did, however, decide that it was worth making the trip in 1981, and again in 1984, but sadly the South Americans prevailed each time.

As everyone knows, the Japanese love football, and each year upwards of 60,000 people have always turned up to see what they hope will be an entertaining game between two of the world's best club sides. They have, however, occasionally been disappointed.

Liverpool fans were certainly disappointed when, at its first attempt, their team lost 3-0 to Flamengo Rio of Brazil in 1981. Three years later the side again found itself in Tokyo, this time going down to a more modest defeat (1-0) at the hands of Independiente of Argentina.

In 2005, the competition was replaced by the Club World Championship, a six-team tournament to feature sides from Africa, Asia, Oceania and Central America. Despite the potential fixture problems their absence would create at home, Liverpool were told they could not withdraw. They slipped to a 1-0 defeat against Sao Paulo in front of a 66,000-plus crowd – a disappointing end to such a brilliant year.

Xabi

Xabier Alonso Olano is the Spanish international with more than 70 caps who is known the football world over as simply Xabi.

His father, Periko, starred for Real Sociedad, Barcelona and Spain, but his son looks likely to eclipse his glorious career. A £10 million buy from Real Sociedad in 2004, Alonso (born on 25 November 1981) had steered his club to second in La Liga behind mighty Real Madrid in 2002-03, receiving a national call-up as a reward for his influence. His debut came at age 21 against Ecuador.

He proved his value to the side by his absence after breaking his ankle against Chelsea on New Year's Day 2005, but recovered to play a part in the run-in to European glory. Alonso missed a pressure penalty in the Final at 2-3 down but recovered quickly enough to net the rebound and set up that nerve-wracking spot-kick shoot-out (in which

ABOVE Xabi Alonso battles with Osman of Everton

he happily didn't have to participate).

"Passing-wise, not many players in Europe are on a level with him," says his former Liverpool team-mate Jamie Carragher. And, after he had played 141 games and 35 games for the Reds, Real Madrid showed that they agreed with Carra when they paid £30m for Xabi in August 2009. Liverpool had lost an influential player, and it is believed that it was behind-the-scenes disagreements with Rafa Benitez that hastened his departure.

Yeats

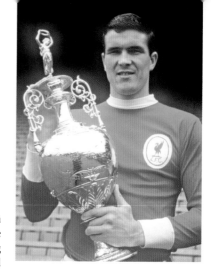

Bill Shankly signed Ron Yeats (born on 15 November 1947) from Dundee United in July 1961 and at his unveiling suggested the press entourage should "take a walk round him". Big Ron, nick-named 'The Colossus' by Shanks, would be a giant figure during a 450-game Liverpool career.

Before any major successes, however, there was the small matter of gaining promotion from the Second Division: Yeats missed only one league match as Liverpool won the title by eight points. Two seasons later, captain Yeats was lift-ing the Division One trophy.

In fact, for a decade Ron was the rock of Liverpool's defence, making the very most of his physique and ability to read a game. In 1965, he became the first Liverpool captain to lift the FA Cup, after a 2-1 extra time victory over Leeds, while another First Division title came

his and Liverpool's way in 1966.

Yeats also led Liverpool in their first forays into Europe, reaching the European Cup semi-finals in 1965, and the Cup Winners' Cup Final in 1966, when they were pipped 2-1 in extra time by Borussia Dortmund.

The 1970s saw Bill Shankly looking to rebuild. Yeats played in all but five League matches in 1969-70, but by then Larry Lloyd was being groomed as his replacement. One of Liverpool's great-est defenders and captains, Yeats moved to Tranmere in 1971 and later became their manager. Later still, in 1986, the Colossus returned to Anfield to become the club's chief scout. He retired after 20 years in the role.

YOU'LL NEVER WALK ALONE

You'll Never Walk Alone

As well as singing the Scouse national anthem, 'Ferry Cross The Mersey', Gerry and the Pacemakers were responsible for popularising 'You'll Never Walk Alone', from the Rodgers and Hammerstein musical Carousel, as a pop song. The Kop adopted it as their anthem, and history was made.

Gerry and the Pacemakers were the first artists to have Number 1 records with their first three releases, and 'You'll Never Walk Alone' was the third, in October 1963. "I'd have made it four with 'I'm The One', says frontman Gerry Marsden now, "but the Searchers (another Liverpool band) stayed on top with 'Needles And Pins'. I kept telling John McNally, John, will you get off the bloody top?"

The mid-1960s was a time when the city of Liverpool simultaneously became the centre of the pop and sporting worlds, Bill Shankly's team giving the crowd something to sing about and many of the songs being supplied by the city's finest groups.

LEFT Gerry Marsden sings "You'll never walk alone" before the FA Cup Final between Liverpool and Everton in 1989

BELOW A flag in Taksim Square, Turkey prior to the Champions League Final, 2005

Marsden has noted the song's affinity with football, at Anfield and elsewhere, and in 1988 recorded a new version of 'You'll Never Walk Alone' to raise funds for the Bradford football ground fire appeal. The Kop's own version was sampled on a 1971 Pink Floyd record, Fearless, and DJ John Peel had it played at his funeral in 2004. You can bet he's not the only one.

A LIVERPOOL A to Z | 139

Youth Team

Liverpool's youth team has the good fortune to operate out of one of the finest football academies in the country. Opened in January 1999, the Liverpool FC Academy in Kirkby represents a £10 million investment by the club.

There are ten grass pitches, four of which are floodlit, and a synthetic pitch made up of rubber granules on a sand base with a two-inch shock absorber underneath that is so realistic it will even take a stud if required.

The academy boasts a state-of-the-art medical and physiotherapy centre, hydrotherapy pool and weights room, together with offices, seminar and dining facilities for staff and students.

Among the players to have emerged from Liverpool's youth system in recent years are Michael Owen (a member of the team that won the FA Youth Cup in 1996), Steve McManaman, Robbie Fowler, Jamie Carragher, Steven Gerrard and Trent Alexander Arnold.

Zero

Keeping goals out was one of the tenets on which Bill Shankly first brought success to Liverpool. It continued under Bob Paisley: Ray Clemence's record of 16 goals conceded in 42 games in 1978-79 and only four games lost was only beaten in 2004-05 by Chelsea's 15 in 38 games.

But fast forward a decade and the number of clean sheets kept in the 1990s was a cause for concern, not least in a disastrous 1998-99 campaign when David James conceded 49 and the club only finished seventh.

The arrival of Dutchman Sander Westerveld in summer 1999 showed new manager Gérard Houllier's determination to tighten up at the back, and in his era the goals conceded column was to be admired rather than laughed at. In Westerveld's first season at the club, Liverpool conceded the least amount of goals in the Premiership (30) that year and finished fourth.

But Houllier moved swiftly after the Dutch keeper blundered against Bolton in August 2001, and a double transfer swoop saw Jerzy Dudek and Chris Kirkland arrive at Anfield on the same day, Westerveld heading for Real Sociedad four months later.

Dudek's 29 clean sheets in his first season helped Liverpool to second place in the Premiership and the UEFA Champions League quarter-finals. A mistake against Manchester United in December 2002 saw Kirkland replace him, but an injury let Dudek back in to excel in the 2003 League Cup final victory against United.

Pepe Reina, who arrived in 2005, kept no fewer than 126 clean sheets in his first 259 appearances for the club and has now played nearly 400 times for the club.

Belgian keeper Simon Mignolet kicked off his first season at Anfield as the Reds' first-choice stopper and enjoyed a dream debut when his penalty save in the closing minutes preserved a 1-0 home triumph over Stoke.

ABOVE Reina saves a penalty from Geremi of Chelsea

BELOW Chris Kirkland gives orders during a match in 2004

**The pictures in this book were provided
courtesy of the following:**

GETTY IMAGES
101 Bayham Street, London NW1 0AG

PA PHOTOS
paphotos.com

WIKICOMMONS
commons.wikimedia.org

Design and artwork by Alex Young

Published by G2 Entertainment Limited

Publishers Jules Gammond and Edward Adams

Written by Jules Gammond

Updated by Rob Mason